THE SELF-EVALUATION FILE

GOOD IDEAS AND PRACTICAL TOOLS FOR TEACHERS, PUPILS AND SCHOOL LEADERS

John MacBeath

John MacBeath is Chair of Educational Leadership at the University of Cambridge.

THE **SELF-EVALUATION** FILE

About the Author

John MacBeath is the Chair of Educational Leadership at the University of Cambridge He is also Director of Learning for Leadership: the Cambridge Network and the Carpe Vitam Centre both based at the University of Cambridge.

From 1997 to 2001 he was a member of the Government's Task Force on Standards and from 1997 to 1999 Scotland's Action Group on Standards. Consultancies have included the Organisation for Economic Co-operation and Development (OECD), UNESCO and ILO (International Labour Organisation), the Education Department of Hong Kong, the Bertelsmann Foundation, the Varkey Group and the European Commission on school self-evaluation and European indicators. He has published extensively on school leadership, school improvement and on school self-evaluation.

About the book

The book is a collection of instruments that have been tried and tested by teachers and pupils and helped to:

- open up new insights into learning and teaching

- promote dialogue between teachers and pupils about learning preferences and styles

- identify how teaching and learning can be made more effective

- raise standards through greater understanding of what it means to be a good student

It also contains tools for school management to take a closer look at:

- the creation and sustaining of a culture of achievement

- the qualities of leadership

- the distinctive roles of management

- priorities in the use of time and the match with personal and professional values

To obtain further copies:

The Self-Evaluation File is published and distributed in the UK by Learning Files Scotland Ltd.
Pollok Castle Estate, Glasgow G77 6NT. Phone 0141 639 5836
Mobile: 07979951858 Fax: 0141 616 3588 E-mail: learningfiles@tiscali.co.uk.

The Self-Evaluation File is distributed in Hong Kong by Mr. S.M. Tsui,
International Network for Educational Improvement, 20 Des Voeux Road, Room 1405
Takshing House, Hong Kong. Phone (852) 2526 8038
Fax: (852) 2526 4705 E-mail: inei@netvigator.com

ISBN No. 0 9543823 0 7

THE SELF-EVALUATION FILE

CONTENTS	PAGE

INTRODUCTION
1. GETTING STARTED 5
2. WHY EVALUATE? 6
3. WHO EVALUATES? 7
4. WHO IS IT FOR? 8

SECTION 1 – LEARNING AND TEACHING
1. THE FORCE FIELD 10
2. THE SPOT CHECK 13
2.1 A VARIATION 15
2.2 GRAPHING A SLICE OF THE SCHOOL DAY 17
2.3 GRAPHING A LESSON 21
3. TEACHING MEETS LEARNING 22
3.1 THE READY-TO-USE QUESTIONNAIRE 23
3.2 THE BLANK FORM 24
4. WORKING WITH OTHERS 26
5. THINKING ABOUT LEARNING 28
6. THE HOMEWORK CHALLENGE 29
7. TRIANGULATING THE EVIDENCE 34
8. SUPPORTING LEARNING AT HOME 36
9. FEEDBACK ON THE TEACHER'S PERFORMANCE 38
10. PRESENTATION AND DISCUSSION 41
11. EVALUATING CLASSROOM MANAGEMENT 42
12. ADDING AND LOSING VALUE 44
13. THE CRITICAL INCIDENT ANALYSIS 45

SECTION 2 – ETHOS AND CULTURE
1. WELCOME FEEDBACK 49
2. ETHOS INDICATORS 51
3. THE CHANGE PROFILE 56
4. ETHOS IN A WORD 60
5. THE SELF-EVALUATION PROFILE 61
6. THE DOUBLE-SIDED QUESTIONNAIRE 64
7. SHOWING THE GAP 66
8. TRIANGULATION 67
9. BENCHMARKING ETHOS 69

SECTION 3 – MANAGEMENT AND LEADERSHIP
1. ME AS I AM/ME AS I WOULD LIKE TO BE 72
2. PIE CHARTS 75
3. THE HEADTEACHER'S 24 HOUR LOG 77
4. THE URGENCY/IMPORTANCE MATRIX 79
5. HOW GOOD IS LEADERSHIP IN OUR SCHOOL? 81
6. HOW GOOD AM I AS A LEADER AND MANAGER? 83
7. FORMAL AND INFORMAL LEADERSHIP 84

THE SELF-EVALUATION FILE

THE **SELF-EVALUATION** FILE

INTRODUCTION

The self-evaluation file is a collection of instruments, or tools, that schools can use to gauge different aspects of their quality and effectiveness. They fall into three main categories:

- **learning and teaching**
- **ethos and culture**
- **leadership and management**

This may be represented as three concentric circles. At the centre is learning - the main and central purpose of the school. The next layer is also crucial because it is about the ethos which makes learning and teaching possible. The third circle is equally vital again because without good management and leadership a school culture will fail to thrive.

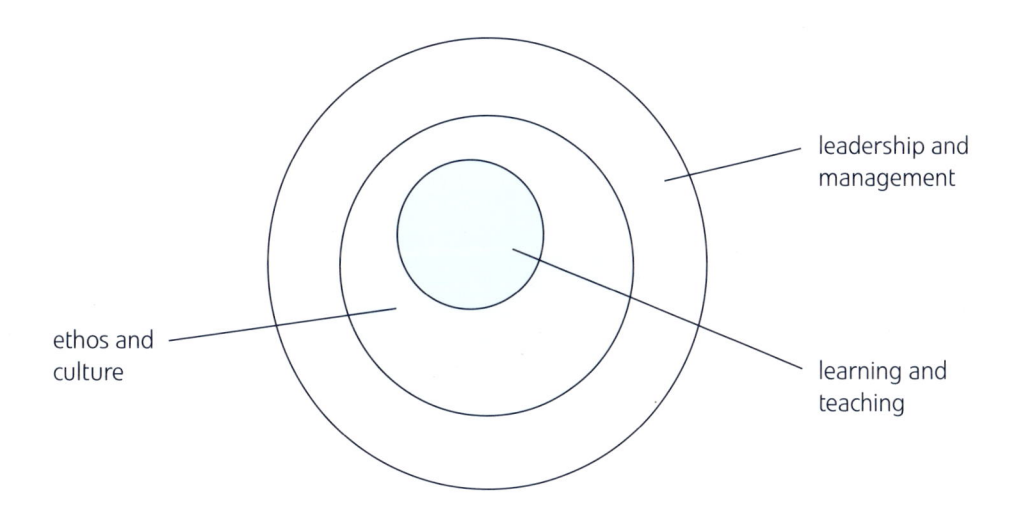

Evaluation is not just about what pupils achieve because ultimately that tells us little about the quality of a school or classroom. What is important for teachers, school leaders, parents and pupils is to keep in touch with learning on continuing basis, and to be alive to the conditions which support and detract from it.

THE **SELF-EVALUATION** FILE

1. GETTING STARTED

Where do you start with the criteria against which a school, or class is measured? The most usual procedure is for policy makers and their advisers to draw up criteria, sometimes with the help of teachers, sometimes piloting these before putting them into operation. It is not surprising then if teachers do not embrace these enthusiastically, as there is no sense of involvement in their creation, no sense of ownership.

Self-evaluation is much more meaningful when those at the receiving end are also at the creation end, discussing and formulating what is important to them - their 'careabouts'. Eliciting careabouts is a fairly simple process but one that brings long term, as well as immediate, rewards.

Different stakeholders want different things from school and have different priorities, but underlying these is a core of common concerns. Recognising these differences is as important as establishing the commonalities. Each group of stakeholders starts from what is of immediate importance to them, moving from their first order priorities to issues affecting them less directly. So teachers may begin with their need for support and for information but then go on to identify pupils' learning needs and expectations. Parents' careabouts always start with the safekeeping and welfare of their own children but then move on to identify wider more inclusive issues.

Teachers' concerns	Management's concerns	Parents' concerns	Pupils' concerns
Support for teaching	Effective leadership	A safe and orderly environment	Teachers who listen to you
Good information and communication flow	A stimulating ethos	Prompt action to deal with problems	Teachers who can control the class
	Good reputation in the community		

2. WHY EVALUATE?

Evaluation is not a one-off event, in preparation for an inspection, an annual audit, an end of term or end of year summary. It is ongoing and everyday. Teachers make a thousand evaluations or more every day, usually intuitively and informally. This selection of tools is designed to lend depth and rigour and value to those evaluations. One single principle guides their selection - the principle of economy and power. The tools in this volume are easy-to-use, often requiring no more than a few minutes or less of a teacher's or pupil's time. They are economic but they are powerful too because they confront big questions and can lead to deep discovery. The principle may be expressed in another way:

> ***tools should be as simple as possible and as complex as necessary.***

While each of the instruments is presented within one of these three contexts all are adaptable to different contexts, and some examples are offered as to ways in which the content may be customised.

THE **SELF-EVALUATION** FILE

3. WHO EVALUATES?

Who evaluates? Whether the focus is on learning, ethos or leadership, who is seen as the most appropriate person or group to conduct an evaluation? Inspectors, headteachers, teachers, pupils, parents, governors or School Boards each bring their own ways of seeing, their own experience and expertise. The following table suggests some of the pluses and minuses of each potential evaluator. It is a useful staff development exercise to give people a blank form and ask them to discuss the pluses and minuses of each. The following list which may be given out as feedback is suggestive rather than definitive and a starter rather than an end point of discussion.

Plus	Minus
The inspector Connoisseurship Training Prior experience Authority	Lack of time High stakes (carrying far-reaching consequences for the school) Lack of contextual knowledge
The headteacher Informal knowledge Authority	Limited time Fairly high stakes Relatively little experience
The teaching colleague Trust Negotiation Reciprocity Knowledge of context	Limited time Limited expertise in evaluation
The teacher herself/himself Self-knowledge Familiarity with the class as individuals Knowledge of context	Familiarity Protection of ego
The pupil Day-to-day knowledge Motivation Time	Lack of authority Little expertise in evaluation Over familiarity with the classroom

4. WHO IS IT FOR?

The nature of evaluation is also determined by who it is for. Evaluations carried out with an inspectorate in mind will be conducted differently and have different results from one intended for teachers. The following table may be used with staff and/or students to identify issues that arise when considering each of the various audiences being reported to.

Audience	Issues to Consider
Parents	
The Education Authority	
School Inspectors	
Pupils	
Teachers	

SECTION 1

LEARNING AND TEACHING

Learning and teaching are often spoken about as if they were the same thing - inseparable twins, yet as we know most learning takes place without teaching and most teaching does not result in learning. So we need instruments which look at both separately but also examine their inter-relationship. No teacher could be satisfied with teaching that did not result in learning and must, in a rapidly changing world, take a close interest in pupils' independent and self-initiated learning.

This section contains 12 instruments some of which take as their focus what the teacher is doing while others focus on what the pupil is doing. Some look from the outside - with a focus on behaviour, while others probe the inside world of thinking and feeling.

Focus	Outside	Inside
Teacher	Teacher performance	My best thinking
Pupil	Working with others (and inside)	Force field
		Spot check
	Thinking about learning (and inside)	Spot check - a variation
		Graphing the school day
	Critical incident analysis	Graphing a lesson
	Adding and losing value	Homework

THE **SELF-EVALUATION** FILE

1. THE FORCE FIELD

This section begins with perhaps the simplest of all tools - the force field. It consists of one single sheet with two sets of three arrows pointing in opposing directions to represent counteracting forces acting on the person, or situation, in the centre. It is simple for the user (pupil or teacher) to simply draw the six arrows on a sheet of paper.

Purpose

The purpose of the force field is to identify those things that help and those things that hinder a pupil's learning. It can be presented in a number of different ways but its depiction below with counteracting arrows suggests that it is a dynamic set of forces acting as brakes and accelerators. Pushing on the accelerator will only drive things forward when the pressure on the brakes is relieved.

Use

Pupils are given the sheet with the two sets of arrows, or are asked to draw them. They are asked, anonymously, to write six things (three brakes, three accelerators) that help and hinder their learning. The context for this needs to be clear, for example:

- in this classroom

- in school generally

- in the library or resource centre

- in study support

- at home

THE **SELF-EVALUATION** FILE

things that help	things that hinder
——————▶	◀——————
——————▶	◀——————
——————▶	◀——————

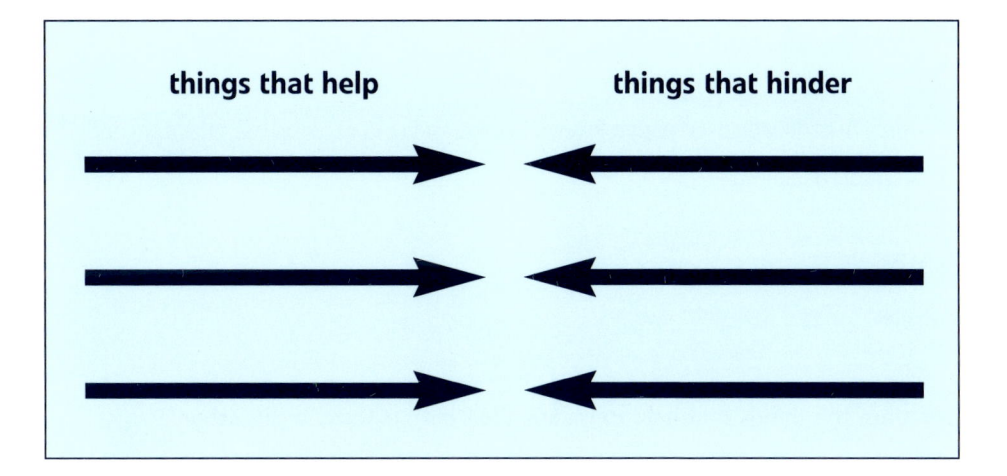

Each different context to which the force field refers will provide different answers and a teacher may choose to explore this range of contexts in order to help pupils understand where and how they learn best.

The sheets may be collected in and compiled to give a whole range of ideas - a class of thirty will generate 180 items in total, usually in the space of about five to ten minutes. This may be done as a group activity rather than simply by individuals, so encouraging pupils to share, discuss, explore the common ground and individual differences.
Below is one example from a class compilation.

HELP

Teachers discussing with you why you are doing things

Helping others and others helping you

Getting help when you are stuck

Getting a chance to have your say

Having music in the class

Doing lots of different activities

Showing how what you learn is useful in real life

Discussing how people learn in their own style

HINDER

Other pupils stopping you working

Being interrupted when you are trying to concentrate

Teachers putting red marks all over your work

Being made fun of - by other pupils or by the teacher

Not being allowed to learn in your own way

Teachers being too strict

Teachers not listening to your opinion

Unfairness and favouritism

THE **SELF-EVALUATION** FILE

Other uses

The force field may be used with a focus on ethos and culture, or on management and leadership. For example:

Culture

What are the things that help to create a learning culture in this school?
- teachers exchanging ideas and practice
- teachers' openness to learning from their pupils
- readiness of everyone to reflect, learn and improve

What are the things that hinder its development?
- defensive attitudes
- lack of time for CPD
- high levels of stress and pressure

Leadership

What are the aspects of leadership that empower teachers?
- trust in teachers' professionalism
- openness to teachers' views
- acknowledgement and understanding of teachers' difficulties

What are the disempowering forces?
- inability to deal with conflicting views
- lack of consultation
- unreasonable demands on teachers and pupils

2. THE SPOT CHECK

The spot check draws on pioneering work by Csikszentmihalyi and Leone and Richards using what is called 'periodic subjective sampling'. They used a simple questionnaire instrument for pupils to fill in at a given point during the day, for example when a buzzer sounded or alerted by a pager which they carried with them, so that whether they were sitting in the classroom, doing homework, watching television, playing chess, walking or riding a bicycle, they would stop to fill in the items on the questionnaire form. This would take no more than two or three minutes and would be done up to eight times day.

Purpose

The purpose of the spot check is to gauge, at an given moment, the emotional and intellectual state of the individual. By examining the profile of the completed questionnaire a judgement could be made as to whether the individual in question was in a state of 'flow' - high engagement/high skill, or experiencing boredom, apathy or anxiety.

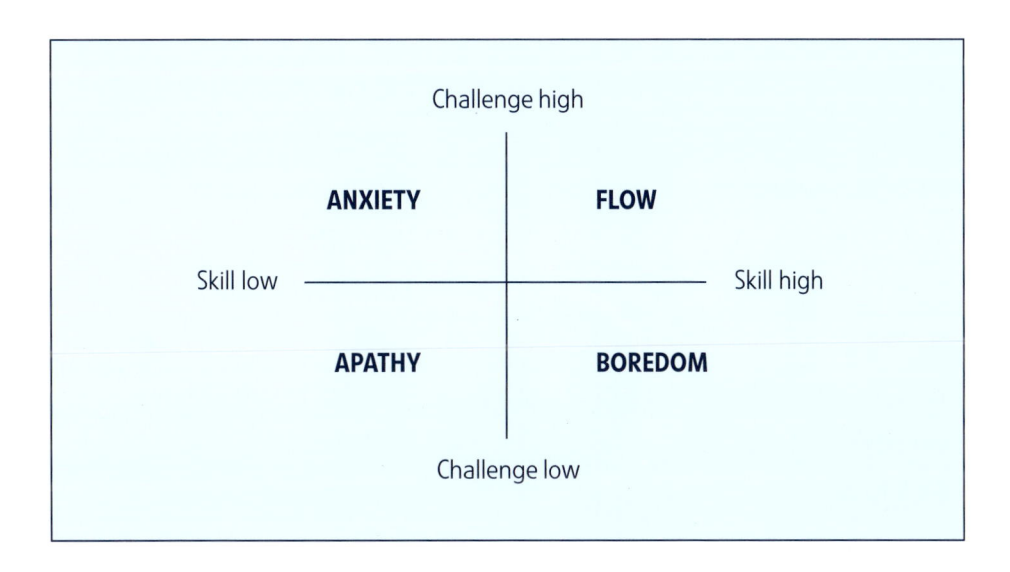

```
                    Challenge high
                         |
         ANXIETY         |      FLOW
                         |
Skill low ───────────────┼─────────────── Skill high
                         |
         APATHY          |     BOREDOM
                         |
                    Challenge low
```

THE **SELF-EVALUATION** FILE

Use

In the school context the spot check has proved an immensely useful tool for teachers and pupils. At a given moment the teacher stops and asks the class to fill in the questionnaire. It is helpful if the pupils have the questionnaire in advance as by the time it is distributed, the immediacy of thinking and feeling will have been lost.

Once it has been filled out the teacher may either:

- collect it in, tally the scores and present it back to the class at a later date for discussion and interpretation
- and/or engage immediately in discussion of some of the 'findings'.

SPOT CHECK

CONCENTRATING	1	2	3	THINKING ABOUT OTHER THINGS
ALERT	1	2	3	DROWSY
RELAXED	1	2	3	ANXIOUS
WISHING TO BE HERE	1	2	3	WISHING TO BE SOMEWHERE ELSE
HAPPY	1	2	3	SAD
ACTIVE	1	2	3	PASSIVE
EXCITED	1	2	3	BORED
TIME PASSING QUICKLY	1	2	3	TIME PASSING SLOWLY
FULL OF ENERGY	1	2	3	VERY LITTLE ENERGY
SOMETHING AT STAKE	1	2	3	NOTHING AT STAKE
SOCIABLE	1	2	3	LONELY
EASY TO CONCENTRATE	1	2	3	DIFFICULT TO CONCENTRATE
CHEERFUL	1	2	3	IRRITABLE
EASY TO BE CREATIVE	1	2	3	DIFFICULT TO BE CREATIVE

2.1. THE SPOT CHECK – A VARIATION

This variation on the spot check was devised by students of the Learning School (see page 16). It adds a prelude and postscript to the instrument, asking the student to note his/her state of mind/feeling before the lesson and then again at the end. These provide the outer ends of the spot check sandwich and so lend an extra dimension to the evaluation.

Purpose

The additional element to the spot check allows teachers and students to explore how expectation and satisfaction are inter-related but also how pupils may be surprised into learning.

Use

Immediately before the lesson starts pupils fill in the 'smiley face' part of the questionnaire and also describe their mood in anticipation. During the lesson at one or more key moments the spot check questionnaire is completed and at the end again the 'smiley face' is filled in.

After collation of the results the data may be fed back to the class as a stimulus to discussion, probing what the data mean and exploring the relationship between expectation and satisfaction

THE **SELF-EVALUATION** FILE

Date: Period

PART 1 - PRE QUESTIONS
Please complete this part before you start your lesson, just circle the answers most relevant to you.

How do you feel at the moment?	too cold bored scared	too hot excited perfect	happy tired	sad hungry	lethargic angry

Are you in the mood for learning this period? ☺₅ ☺₄ 😐₃ ☹₂ 😖₁

PART II - SPOT CHECK
Please complete this section when instructed to do so by either the teacher or a student researcher.

ARE YOU...

concentrating	3	2	1	thinking about other things
alert	3	2	1	drowsy
relaxed	3	2	1	anxious
wishing to be here	3	2	1	wishing to be somewhere else
happy	3	2	1	sad
active	3	2	1	passive
excited	3	2	1	bored
time passing quickly	3	2	1	time passes slowly
full of energy	3	2	1	very little energy
sociable	3	2	1	lonely
easy to concentrate	3	2	1	difficult to concentrate
cheerful	3	2	1	irritable
productive	3	2	1	difficult to be productive
willing to participate	3	2	1	not willing to participate
motivated	3	2	1	discouraged

PART III - POST QUESTIONS
This section should be completed at the end of the lesson just before you leave the class.

How much did you learn during the lesson? ☺₅ ☺₄ 😐₃ ☹₂ 😖₁
                                            A Lot   Not Much

How much did you chat during the lesson? ☺₅ ☺₄ 😐₃ ☹₂ 😖₁

Thank you very much for taking the time to complete this questionnaire.
Please leave it on your desk as you leave the class.

2.2. GRAPHING A SLICE OF A SCHOOL DAY

Purpose

This adaptation of the spot check is designed to give a view of one student's engagement with what is being taught over the course of a school day. It compares levels of expectation before each period with student satisfaction at some point during the lesson..

Use

The student is asked to rate his/her motivation at the start of the lesson, using a four point scale. The student continues to complete this at agreed intervals - for example every 10 or 20 minutes. At the same time student rates his/her learning, also on a four point scale. For any one student this can be converted on to a chart such as those on the following pages. The first shows a rising and falling expectation score over the course of the day. The second graph shows learning as rated by the student. The third puts motivation and learning together on the same graph. The spot check may be used to give a more in depth picture of what the student is doing/thinking/feeling at any given time. As with all data on motivation learning the graph is only the starting point for dialogue with the individual student or with the whole class.

THE **SELF-EVALUATION** FILE

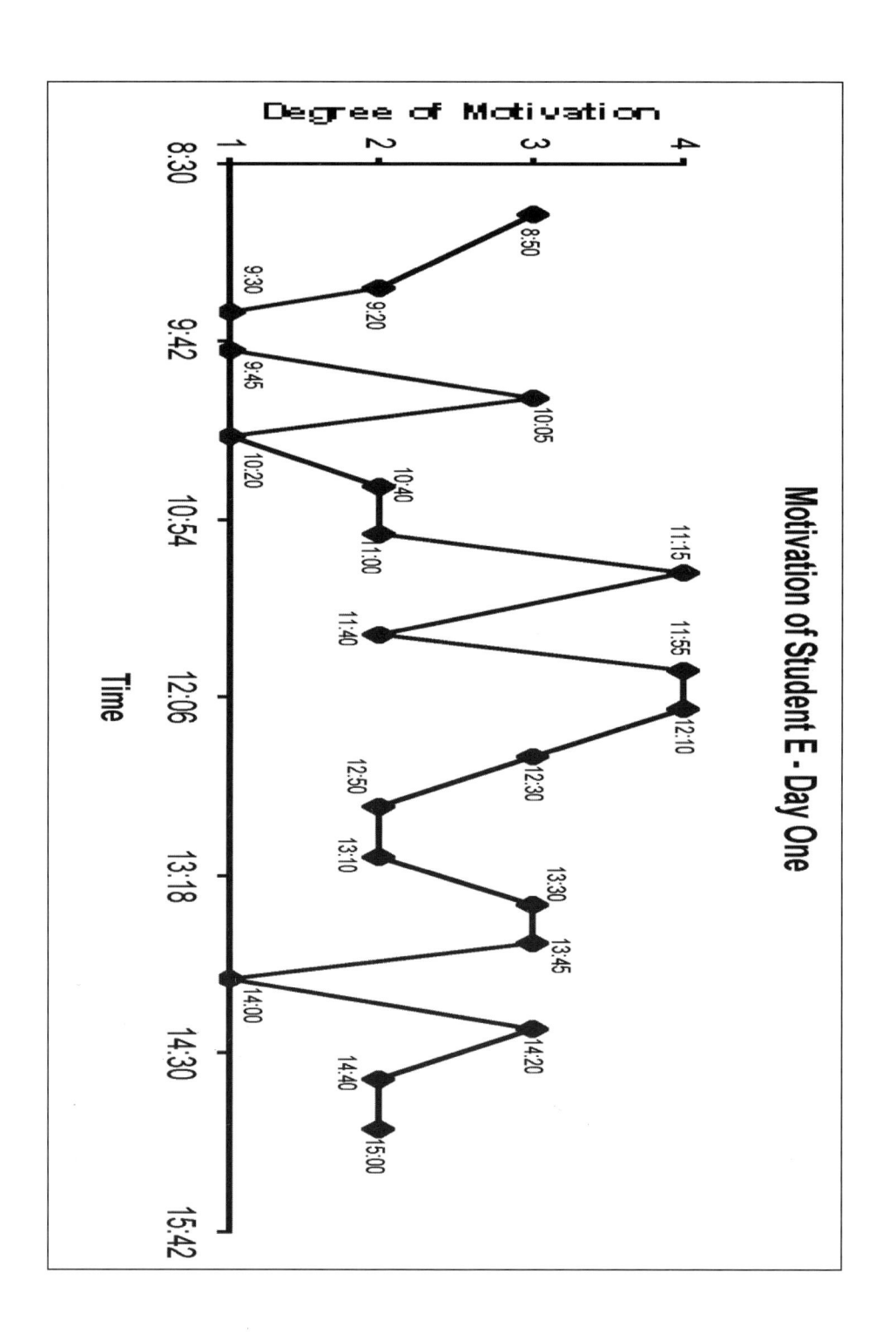

Motivation of Student E - Day One

THE **SELF-EVALUATION** FILE

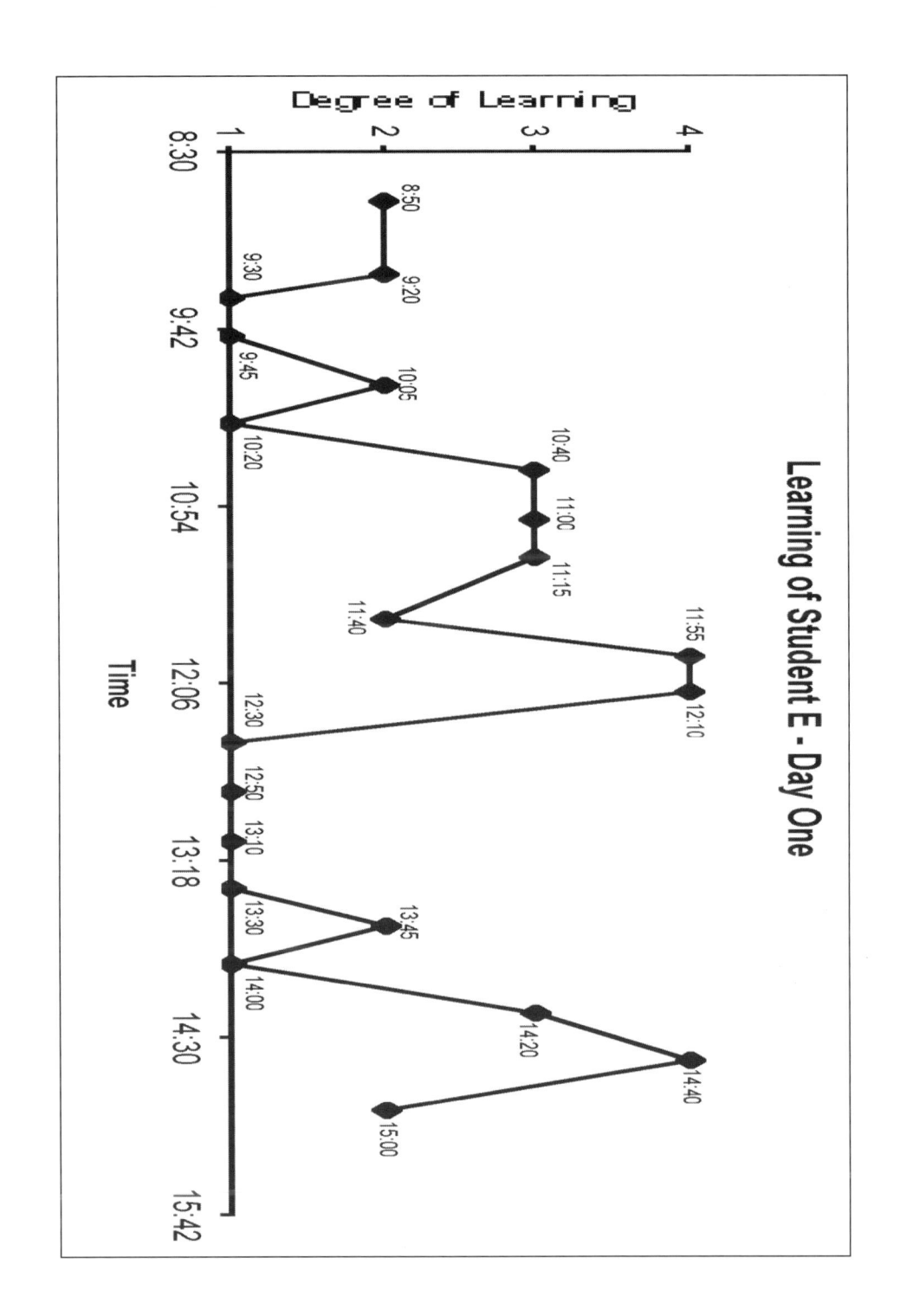

Learning of Student E - Day One

THE **SELF-EVALUATION** FILE

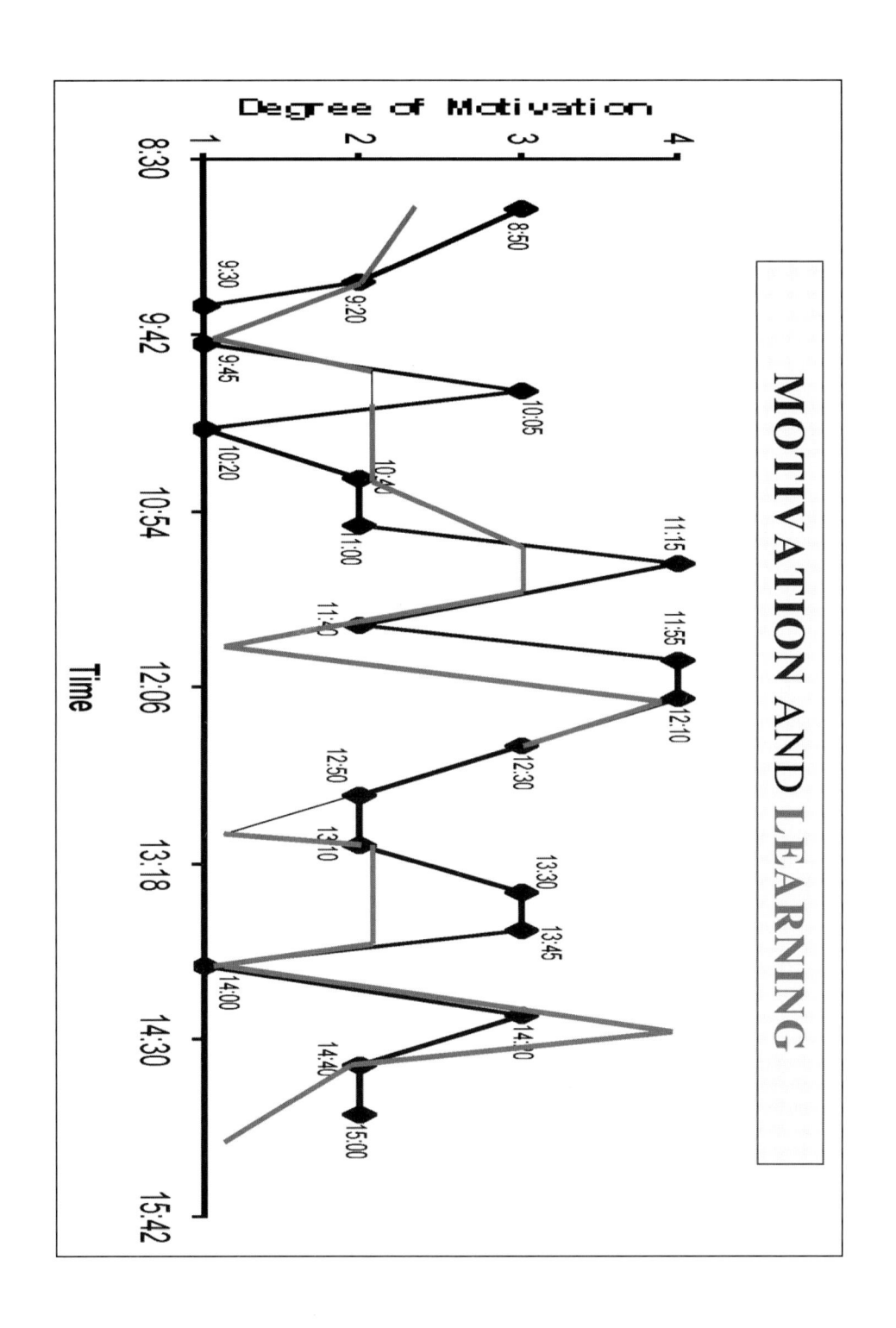

MOTIVATION AND LEARNING

20

2.3 GRAPHING A LESSON

Purpose

This further variation on the spot check is designed to get a closer view of a student's engagement over the course of one specific lesson. It illustrates what kind of activity is most and least engaging, most and least likely to be a 'flow' experience.

Use

The spot check is used six times at regular intervals and the results noted against what was happening at each of those six occasions. The example below illustrates one student's experience.

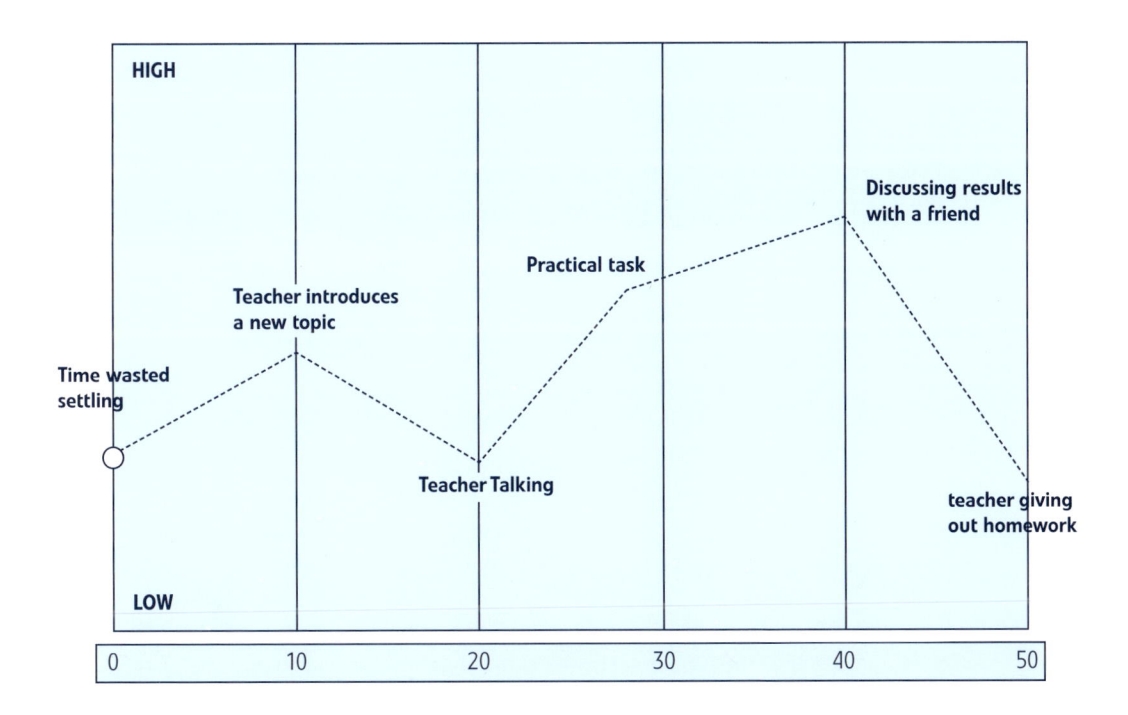

3. TEACHING MEETS LEARNING

This instrument is a questionnaire with two sets of responses, one about frequency of use of a particular classroom methodology, the other response indicating the extent to which it promotes learning. The responses are graphed on a two dimensional model showing where the greatest congruence and discrepancies lie.

Purpose

The instrument is designed to:

- evaluate the extent to which pupils feel that various classroom methodologies contribute to their own learning
- help the teacher adjust teaching strategies in the light of pupil feedback.

Use

Teachers may use a schedule with pre-prepared categories, or, to give a greater sense of ownership, use it as a class exercise, getting pupils to generate the items which will be used.

Both schedules are shown on the following pages.

THE **SELF-EVALUATION** FILE

3.1 THE READY-TO-USE QUESTIONNAIRE

This example uses familiar categories and although not all categories may be relevant to every classroom the table may be used as a model to introduce pupils to the exercise suggested on the previous page in creating their own protocol.

very often	quite often	only some-times	rarely or never	**Teaching methods**	really learn a lot	learn quite a lot	learn a little	learn nothing
				listening to the teacher				
				answering teacher's questions				
				doing experiments				
				working on the computer				
				watching a video				
				listening to a tape				
				acting out a role play				
				working in pairs				
				working in a group				
				taking notes while the teacher talks				
				taking notes from a book or worksheet				
				making things (like models)				

THE **SELF-EVALUATION** FILE

3.2 THE BLANK FORM

This may be filled in as a class activity. Pupils brainstorm all the different methods used in class then categorise them and enter them in the appropriate place under Teaching Methods.

very often	quite often	only some-times	rarely or never	**Teaching methods**	really learn a lot	learn quite a lot	learn a little	learn nothing

THE **SELF-EVALUATION** FILE

Here is an example of the combined responses from one class, placed on a graph to show the relationship between perceived effectiveness (vertical axis) and frequency of use of that method (horizontal axis).

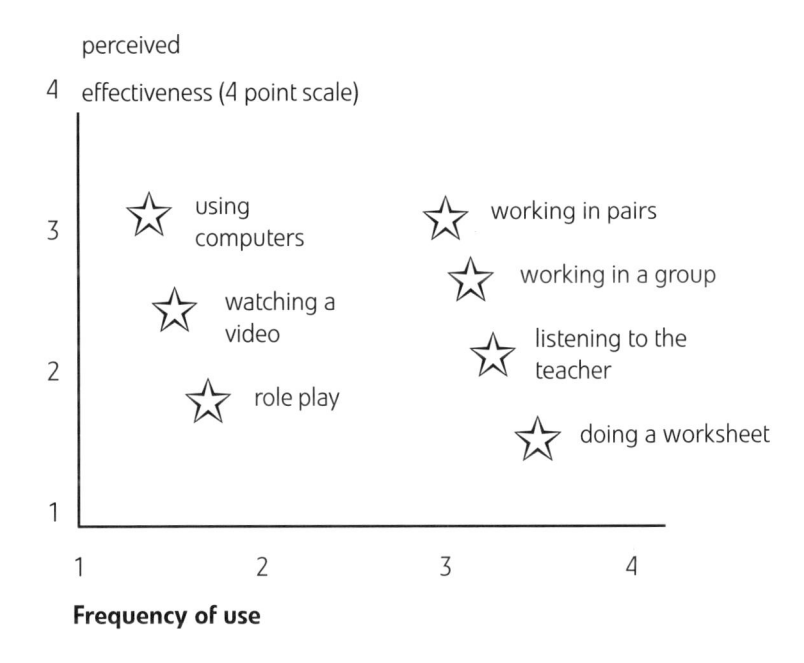

```
perceived
4   effectiveness (4 point scale)

3       ☆ using              ☆ working in pairs
          computers
                              ☆ working in a group
        ☆ watching a
          video               ☆ listening to the
2                               teacher
        ☆ role play
                              ☆ doing a worksheet
1
    1       2         3         4
Frequency of use
```

Like all the examples shown here, this is not an end point, but a starting point for a classroom conversation, leading to an agreement about how classroom teaching and learning can be organised most effectively for everyone.

THE **SELF-EVALUATION** FILE

4. WORKING WITH OTHERS

This questionnaire is designed to be completed by the teacher and by the individual pupil as a starting point for examining and discussing how well and effectively pupils co-operate in the classroom and learn from one another. Teachers and pupils agree beforehand on a scoring system.

Purpose

The primary uses of the instrument are to:

- promote pupil-self assessment, embedding this in normal classroom practice

- raise pupils' awareness of how well they work with others

- open discussion of more effective ways of working in the classroom.

Uses

The teacher explains the purpose of the instrument and asks pupils to take ten minutes or so to fill it out. The teacher explains that he/she will also complete it on their behalf and that they will then have a discussion and try to reach an agreement on what pupils are already good at and what they need to work on in the future.

THE **SELF-EVALUATION** FILE

WORKING WITH OTHERS

	SELF-EVALUATION		TEACHER EVALUATION		SCORE
	good at this	I will still keep trying	good at this	Keep practising	
taking turns					
sharing with others					
letting others have their say					
listening attentively offering to help others having difficulties					
following directions sticking with the task (even when stuck)					
using time well					
looking after materials					
not getting distracted					
explaining how to do things					
accepting responsibility helping others stay on task					
respecting opinions and views different from mine					

THE **SELF-EVALUATION** FILE

5. THINKING ABOUT LEARNING

This is a similar instrument to 'working with others' and is used in the same way except that its focus is on learning and is aimed at assessing the pupil's own learning style, strengths and weaknesses, with a view to working on these individually and as a class.

	SELF-EVALUATION		TEACHER EVALUATION		SCORE
	in general	this lesson	in general	this lesson	
I concentrate on what I am expected to learn					
I take notes of key points					
I try to understand					
I think through the problem carefully					
I explain it to myself to understand it better					
I identify blocks or difficulties with learning					
I ask myself questions about what I'm learning					
I leave a problem and come back to it later					
I look for someone who can help me					
I explain to others what I am learning					
I work hard at overcoming difficulties					
I relate what I am learning to my experience					
I am able to ignore distractions					
I try to relate it to things I've learned before					
I look for someone who can help me					
I try to make the subject matter interesting					
I experiment with ways of memorising things well					

THE SELF-EVALUATION FILE

6. THE HOMEWORK CHALLENGE

The test of how well pupils have acquired learning skills and study habits is what they do when left to their own devices. Without this carry over from classroom to home and home to classroom, learning how to learn may be taught but not learned, practised in school but not practised out of school.

Purpose

The purpose of these instruments is to help young people reflect on their approach to homework for their own benefit and as feedback to teachers so that teachers are in a better position to understand and to support what the quality of learning is like when they are not present.

Uses

This section contains three separate instruments which serve different purposes. These are:

- The homework questionnaire
- The study habits checklist
- The daily log

The homework questionnaire is primarily for the teacher to get feedback from a class on their attitudes to homework, their motivation and their commitment. It provides a starting point for discussion on how homework might be made more engaging and useful. Its best use is by an individual teacher with his or her own class.

The study habit checklist may also be used in the same way but its primary purpose is for the individual student to keep as an aide-memoire, a checklist to refer to on a continuing basis.

The daily log also serves this dual purpose. It is a useful reflective tool for the pupil but also an important source of information for the teacher. Its best use is for a given period - say a week- in which the pupil is asked to keep a faithful record - over seven days - of what he or she did, time spent on it, difficulties encountered and help received. Each pupil needs, therefore, to receive a 7 page log, preferably attractively presented (perhaps a different colour paper for each day) and asked to use it first for their own reference and secondly to hand it in, anonymously, at the end of the week to allow the teacher (or teachers, if used across a whole year group) to review and discuss the implications.

THE **SELF-EVALUATION** FILE

HOMEWORK QUESTIONNAIRE

The purpose of this questionnaire is to help us find out more about what pupils think about homework and to help us make it more enjoyable and useful

Please go through the questionnaire and put a tick in the box which fits what you think. For example, if you enjoy homework just some of the time put a tick in the box under the heading 'sometimes'.

THANK YOU VERY MUCH FOR HELPING US WITH THIS

	all the time	most of the time	sometimes	never
I enjoy doing homework				
I get too much homework				
I get too little homework				
I worry because I can't do the work				
The teacher explains clearly what we have to do for homework				
I use my homework diary				
The teacher forgets to ask for completed homework				
The teacher makes helpful comments about homework after I've done it.				

My parent(s) help me with my homework

My parent(s) give me encouragement with my homework

For me the best thing about homework is: ....

....

For me the worst thing about homework is: ....

....

One word I would use to describe homework is: ....

THE **SELF-EVALUATION** FILE

**Here are some things that young people have said about homework. You may or may not agree.
Tick one of the four boxes to show your own opinion.**

	strongly agree	agree	disagree	strongly disagree
"When I am studying or doing homework I use techniques that really help me to learn things"				
"Homework helps me relate what I am learning in the class to real life situations"				
"I find it difficult to study for exams because things just won't stay in my head"				
"I would find it easier if I could do homework or study with my friends"				
"Homework is so boring I just get it over with as quickly as possible"				
"I find it difficult to concentrate"				
"I often do school work at home even when there is no homework"				
"I wish someone would give me advice on how to plan/organise my homework"				

HOMEWORK				
	less than 1/2 hour	1/2 - 1 hour	1 1/2 - 2 hours	more than 2 hours
On a typical night I do homework ...				
Last night the total time in spent on homework was ...				

THE **SELF-EVALUATION** FILE

STUDY HABITS CHECKLIST

Name ....   date ....

Many learning problems can be helped through the use of good study habits. Good study habits can help you to be successful in school. Use the list below to check your study habits. Put a tick in the column to indicate your answer and be honest with yourself. You may asked to complete the checklist again at a later date.

	Yes	Sometimes	No
I am happy with my study habits			
It's difficult for me to get down to homework or studying			
I am easily put off or distracted			
I have a place where I enjoy working			
I reward myself when I have done something well			
I study or do homework at a time which suits me			
I do urgent or important work first			
I usually leave things to the last minute			
I waste time looking for books, pens, etc.			
I use my diary to note homework and dates in the school calendar			
I use different ways of memorising things			
I use mind mapping			
I can find information I need on the Internet			
I take frequent breaks and work in short bursts			
I take notes that are easy to understand			
I rush when reading instructions and don't always understand them			
I can follow spoken instructions given by teachers			
When I don't understand I phone a friend			
I know how to use a library.			
I ask myself questions about what I am learning			
I leave studying for tests until the last minute			
I often just give up when I get stuck			

THE **SELF-EVALUATION** FILE

Daily Log by ....

In class... date ....

Below is an example of how to fill in our daily diary. Please fill in one of these sheets for each day during the chosen week. If there is not enough room please continue on the back of the page.

Time	Homework	Time spent	Type of Work	Any difficulty	Help?
4.30pm	French	40 minutes	doing an interpretation	yes, didn't understand some of the questions	yes, my mum

Time	Homework	Time spent	Type of Work	Any difficulty	Help?

Time	Other activities, eg: watching TV, washing up, reading a book	Time spent	Who did you do this with?

THE **SELF-EVALUATION** FILE

7. TRIANGULATING THE EVIDENCE

It is good research and evaluation practice to look for more than one source of evidence. Triangulation is when three sources are compared to test whether there is agreement or so that the evidence may be regarded as reliable. One form of triangulation is to compare views of teachers, pupils and parents on a given issue. So, for example, in collecting evidence on homework the same question may be put to all three groups.

For example, these are some questions on homework that may be used by pupils, teachers and parents.

	strongly agree	agree	disagree	strongly disagree
Homework is usually enjoyable				
Homework is suited to individual pupils' needs				
Pupils' views on homework are listened to and taken seriously				
Teachers give feedback on completed homework				
Homework is spread evenly across the week				
Parents are given helpful advice on how to support their children with homework				
Homework helps to overcome difficulties with learning				

THE **SELF-EVALUATION** FILE

The following is an example from one school which triangulates the views of three parties. Examining the differences in view in this school led to a revising of homework policy and practice.

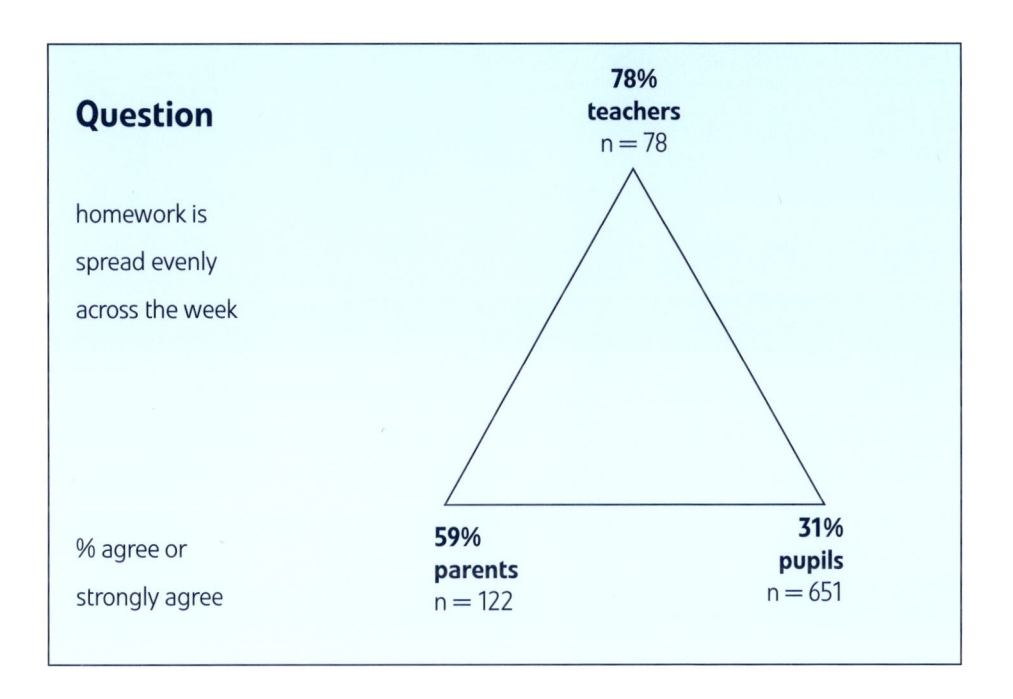

Question

homework is spread evenly across the week

% agree or strongly agree

- 78% teachers n = 78
- 59% parents n = 122
- 31% pupils n = 651

8. SUPPORTING LEARNING AT HOME

Parents can play a valuable role in supporting children's homework and learning at home. However, they often don't know what to do, often fall back on very traditional ways of helping or coaching their children, or give in to their children who get irritated by their 'interference'. So props or prompts which help parents to have a dialogue with their children and evaluate how they learn can relieve the burden and anxiety .

Purpose

The 'supporting learning' grid is just one example of how themes being dealt with in school can carry over into the home context and can be used by parents and children together to develop and evaluate skills and understanding. One of the implicit messages is that literacy, numeracy, and other school 'subjects' are not discrete compartments but have something to do with real life and are learned and rehearsed best in real life contexts.

Uses

The grid provides simply five examples of typical household activities. It asks the parent (perhaps parent and child together) to think of ways in which they can use these events to make connections with what is taught in school and to practise skills that improve thinking, reading or calculation, for example. Having practised it once this may start a conversation which evaluates the effectiveness of what has been done:

- What did we learn?
- How do we know we learned it?
- How could we develop that learning further?
- What else could we do to practise learning in a fun way?

SUPPORTING LEARNING AT HOME

The event	Social studies history, Economics Geography	Literacy and Language	Numeracy, Maths and Science	Art and music	Citizenship Personal and Social Education
	Finding places on the map. Calculating distances and modes of travel.	Reading, talking, listening, discussing.	Adding, multiplying, dividing. Converting currencies. Reading timetables. Calculating times and time differences.	Local customs and cultures. What leisure and cultural events are there?	Developing social and life skills. Considering others' point of view. Weighing up evidence. Making decisions.
You have brochures from a travel agent and are planning a holiday abroad. You look for the best value and most convenient time of travel.					
You are watching ads on TV. You discuss what they are trying to 'sell' and how effective they are, giving marks out of 10 for artistic impression, technical quality, persuasiveness.					
You do a family tree. How far back can you go? How could you find out more? What would the family have been doing 50 years ago? 100 years ago?					
On a car or train journey you are playing 'Who am I?' You choose famous people and have 20 questions to find out the name.					
You are shopping together in the supermarket. Father needs low cholesterol food and Mother is trying to lose weight. What are the best buys?					

37

THE **SELF-EVALUATION** FILE

9. FEEDBACK ON THE TEACHER'S PERFORMANCE

Teachers rarely like having their performance evaluated. It may bring back memories of their college days when assessment by tutors was fraught with anxiety and was high stakes in terms of their future. Their other experiences of evaluation were by inspectors or appraisers - also high stakes and often failing to represent the day to day work of the classroom. Feedback from the class, on the other hand, can be much less intimidating and even very rewarding as long as a climate is created in which:

- pupils feel that their views are valued and will be taken seriously
- teachers have a genuine desire to know how they are perceived by their pupils

The instrument here is one devised by teachers in a German school (Schwalmstadt), used on a voluntary and anonymous basis by teachers and with these safeguards and no coercion. In that school 78% of staff participated.

Purpose

The instrument is designed to give a view - for the teacher and the class - of the teacher's effectiveness across a number of aspects of teaching. With these data, displayed on an overhead transparency, or printed out for the class in graphic form, the teacher and pupils may embark on a discussion of what might be done by both parties to improve the climate for successful learning. This does require the teacher and class to have established a good trusting relationship in which there is a joint ownership of the exercise, preceded by discussion of its value and purpose.

THE **SELF-EVALUATION** FILE

Use

The teacher opens a discussion with the class on teaching styles and methods and explains how difficult it is for a teacher to know what works best without some form of feedback. Pupils are encouraged to be honest and are assured that the feedback is anonymous and they don't have to put their names on it. They are then given the questionnaire and fill it out individually, anonymously, and without consultation. It should take no more than 15 minutes or so but needs to be done without rush and pressure and preferably setting the scene and explaining its formative purpose.

The following items from the German questionnaire may need to be amended to fit a particular classroom context.

> My teacher prepares his lessons well
> My teacher uses a variety of teaching methods
> His/her teaching is clear and understandable
> I feel I am learning useful things
> Tests are given back on time
> My teacher has a good knowledge of his/her subject
> His/her teaching is lively/inspiring
> He/she is quite "human"
> She/he has a good sense of humour
> He/she starts lessons on time
> He/she accepts us as individuals and is interested in our problems
> She/he puts pressure on us to work well
> He/she doesn't ignore us when we put up our hands
> He/she makes use of our contributions
> She/he shows that she values what we have to say
> She/he tries involve all pupils in the lesson
> He/she is fair in his/her marking
> She/he is open to criticism and does not pretend to be perfect
> Her/his class management leads to unrest
> I would like to have this teacher again next year

THE SELF-EVALUATION FILE

THE QUESTIONNAIRE TEMPLATE

	strongly agree	agree	disagree	strongly disagree

THE SELF-EVALUATION FILE

10. PRESENTATION AND DISCUSSION

The presentation of data is shown below. The 4 point scale is shown on the left hand side of the graph. The vertical line shows the range of responses, illustrating the important point that pupils do not always experience the teacher in the same way. The classroom is a different place for different pupils. The spot on the vertical line marks the average or mean when all scores have been computed.

Time is needed for exploration of these data with the class, non-defensively, seeking to understand what the data mean and looking to pupils for explanation and clarification. Embedded in the exercise are some important learning points about statistics, data presentation, and concepts such as 'aggregation', 'mean', and 'variance'.

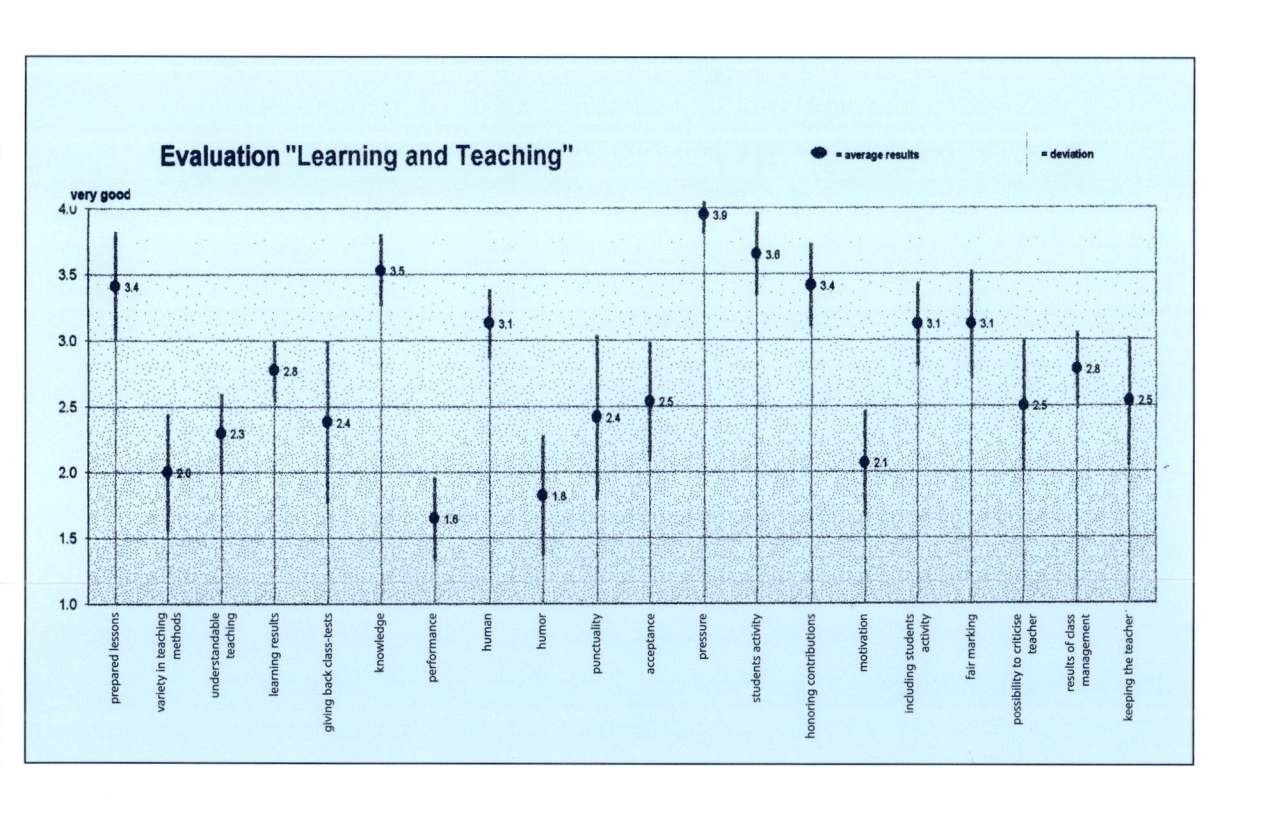

Evaluation "Learning and Teaching"

● = average results | = deviation

Category	Mean
prepared lessons	3.4
variety in teaching methods	2.0
understandable teaching	2.3
learning results	2.8
giving back class-tests	2.4
knowledge	3.5
performance	1.6
human	3.1
humor	1.8
punctuality	2.4
acceptance	2.5
pressure	3.9
students activity	3.6
honoring contributions	3.4
motivation	2.1
including students activity	3.1
fair marking	3.1
possibility to criticise teacher	2.5
results of class management	2.8
keeping the teacher	2.5

41

THE SELF-EVALUATION FILE

11. EVALUATING CLASSROOM MANAGEMENT

One of the most insightful texts and pieces of research into what teachers do was conducted by Kounin in 1970, emanating in a list of things that teachers typically do in classrooms. He invented a new lexicon of terms to describe these actions (shown in the box on the facing page). These offer the ingredients of an observation schedule which can be used in peer mentoring or by student observers who have been trained in observation skills.

Purpose

The seven Kounin categories are essentially an awareness raising list. They alert the teacher to things that he or she may do usually unconsciously. Sometimes very helpfully and sometimes unhelpfully for their students.

Uses

It can be used by the teacher to monitor his/her own behaviour. It can be used in peer observation or coaching where one teacher feeds back to the other on these seven categories, perhaps even scoring the number of occasions when these things are observed or noting the context in which they happen and/or consequences of that action.

A teacher may also use these as a basis for discussion with a class, alerting them to what is more and less helpful for their learning.

Dimensions of classroom management

With-it-ness - An awareness of events going on around even though not directly visible e.g. teacher at blackboard with her back to the class says "Get on with your work Angela"

Overlapping - when the teacher has two or more things to deal with simultaneously e.g. while engaged in one-to-one tuition also signals disapproval (a 'desist' to a misbehaving group)

Dangles - when a teacher starts an activity then leaves it hanging e.g. teacher starts reading from a book then stops to attend to some behavioural issue

Flip-flops - when a teacher starts an activity, then begins another, then returns to the first e.g. teacher says to pupils to put away spelling and get out arithmetic books, then asks pupils about their spelling

Thrusts - when the teacher interrupts pupil activities, perhaps without sensitivity to the group, or individual's readiness e.g. pupils are working in pairs and the teacher stops their activity to address the whole class

Overdwelling when a teacher stays on one issue beyond what was necessary or engaging e.g. teacher goes back repeatedly over the same ground, resulting in some pupils, most, or all becoming bored and disengaged

Fragmentation - when the teacher slows down the pace of the lesson by breaking her instructions into small units instead of a whole e.g. the teacher takes five minutes to get pupils to change from one activity to the next by a series of detailed over elaborate steps

THE **SELF-EVALUATION** FILE

12. ADDING AND LOSING VALUE

Much of school self-evaluation focuses on pupil performance data, comparing outcomes or measuring added value over a given period of time. Every school now has such pupil performance data but find that it is only the beginning of the story. Data provided by tests is summative. It shows what a pupil has achieved at one, two or more points and can show that pupil's gain in performance relative to classmates.

The regression line is the line of the prediction represented by Shahid whose performance on his baseline assessment predicts where he will be at a later point. He neither falls short of nor exceeds prediction. Celeste has a low score to begin with but performs well beyond expectation, while Sadie who started well fails to make predicted progress.

Data such as that shown below needs then to be probed with finer grained instruments to discover why this should be so, enlisting the pupil's help in interpreting the data and researching cause and effect.

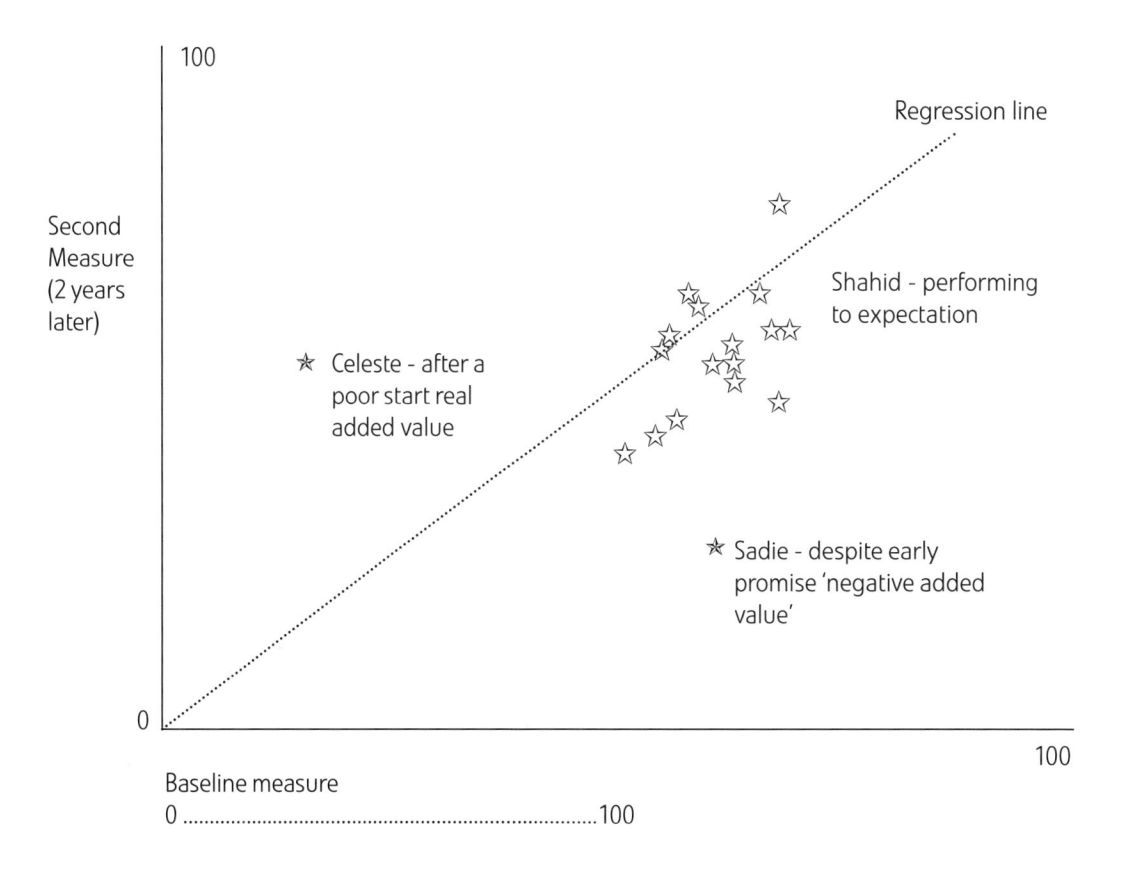

13. THE CRITICAL INCIDENT ANALYSIS

This is a multi purpose instrument that may be used in a number of different contexts and with different foci and purposes. In the example illustrated here, its focus is on the classroom and pupil's interpretations of causes of 'trouble'.

Purpose

The analyses of critical incidents are designed to examine how events arise and how the same thing may be prevented in the future. It serves to give pupils a greater sense of ownership and responsibility for making classroom life more congenial and effective for all.

Use

The teacher introduces the exercise, explaining its purpose. Pupils are asked to work in small groups and to identify a recent incident that had a bad outcome. They are shown how to analyse it as show in the accompanying diagram. They are asked to trace back to the initial causes of the event, to identify the various 'players' and what they did, or didn't do, to contribute to the outcome.

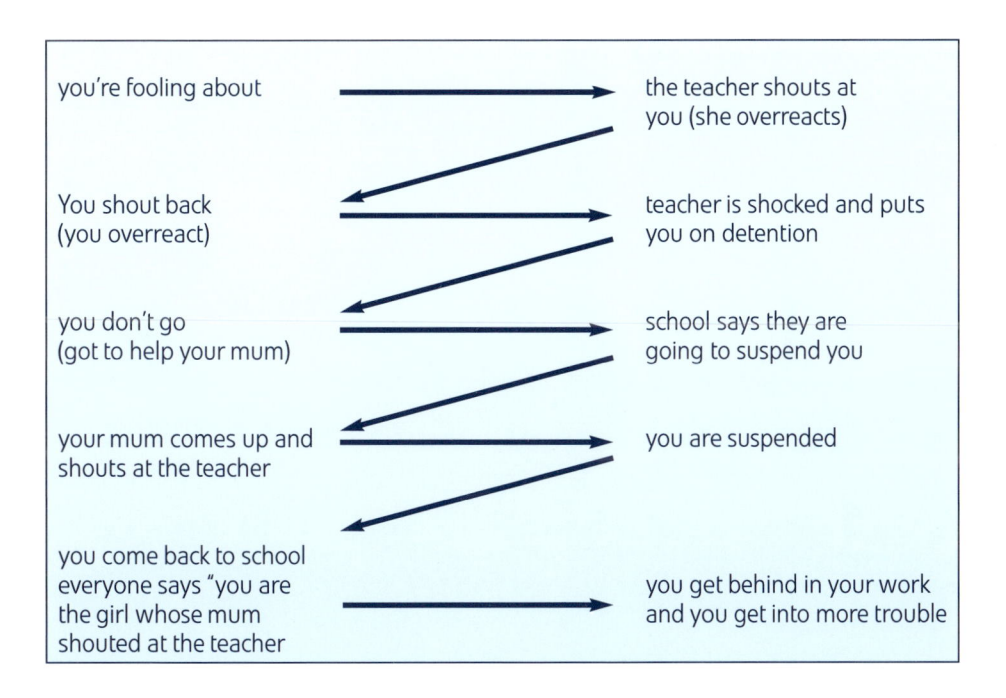

you're fooling about →	the teacher shouts at you (she overreacts)
You shout back (you overreact) ←	teacher is shocked and puts you on detention
you don't go (got to help your mum) →	school says they are going to suspend you
your mum comes up and shouts at the teacher →	you are suspended
you come back to school everyone says "you are the girl whose mum shouted at the teacher →	you get behind in your work and you get into more trouble

45

THE **SELF-EVALUATION** FILE

Stage 2

Having 'unpacked' what actually happened the next stage is to answer these questions:

- How might it have ended differently?
- Who might have behaved differently?
- What might they have done or not done?
- What can we learn from this?
- What do we do next?

THE SELF-EVALUATION FILE

SECTION TWO

ETHOS AND CULTURE

The terms **ethos** and **culture** are often used interchangeably. It is helpful, however, to distinguish the two. Ethos may be seen as the outer face presented to the world, to the parent or the visitor. It is often the immediate 'feel' of the place when you walk through the door for the first time. Culture is deeper lying and is made up of the disparate elements that pupils bring with them from home and community, and the attitudes that teachers too bring with them through the school door. As these 'inputs' interact something new emerges, a unique culture which continues to take shape and change as deliberate efforts are made to forge a learning culture, a democratic culture or a culture of achievement.

The school may be seen a bit like an onion, made up of layers with a core at the centre representing its essential values and beliefs. Beyond that core are overlays of norms, rules, sanctions, and the face that the school presents to the outside world - the school as its exists on paper, in data, statistics and, sometimes, a promotional gloss.

Evaluating the culture of the school may be seen as a process of peeling back the layers, starting with the school on paper, how it documents itself and communicates its beliefs and values to parents, to a wider public and to inspectors and validating agencies such as Investors in People.

As self-evaluation probes deeper it examines the day to day operation of the school and how it maintains order and behaviour through rules, rewards, and sanctions. It seeks to find out not only how effective these are but how they are reflected in the norms of the school ("the way we do things round here") and, at the deeper level, how aligned these are with values and purposes.

THE **SELF-EVALUATION** FILE

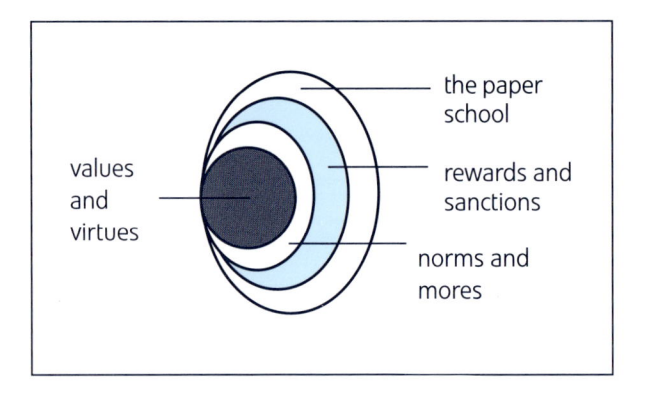

[Diagram: concentric ovals labelled from outer to inner — "the paper school", "rewards and sanctions", "norms and mores", "values and virtues"]

The 7 instruments in section 2 are all designed to help peel back the layers of the school culture, to probe deeper.

	Group	Individual
	Ethos indicators	Ethos in a word
		The double-sided questionnaire
	The self-evaluation profile	Triangulating the evidence
	Welcome feedback	A primary example

48

1. WELCOME FEEDBACK

For the parent visiting the school, perhaps, for the first time, the impressions they get will be strong, often indelible and carry great weight in their evaluation of the school or their choice of the school for their children. The key things that influence their judgement are relationships, communication and being made to feel welcome and wanted.

Purpose

The feedback form gives school management, support staff and teachers an external eye assessment of the school as a welcoming, or less than welcoming, place. It may carry far-reaching implications for school roles and teacher recruitment.

Uses

This short easy-to-complete feedback form takes no more than a minute to complete, As in hotels or airlines, for example, multiple copies can be left in the reception area with a clearly marked box in which to place the completed form. Ensuring a regular supply of pencils or pens is important as many are likely to depart with the last user. Having the school name on them then ensures some free publicity. Tying them down as in banks or post offices is, of course, an option.

THE **SELF-EVALUATION** FILE

WELCOME FEEDBACK

We have tried to make our school a warm and welcoming place. We want to make it better still. We would, therefore, very much value your honest feedback. Could you please take a minute or so to fill in the following form? Thank you.

	yes	no	not relevant
I felt welcome in the school	☐	☐	☐
There was clear signposting to where I wanted to go	☐	☐	☐
Office staff were helpful	☐	☐	☐
I liked the displays of pupils' work	☐	☐	☐
I was kept waiting for a long time without an explanation	☐	☐	☐
There was somewhere comfortable to sit while I was waiting	☐	☐	☐
There was interesting reading material available	☐	☐	☐
Pupils said hello or smiled	☐	☐	☐

Please write one word to describe your impressions on entering the school

Do you have any suggestions as to how we might improve things for parents or other visitors to the school?

2. ETHOS INDICATORS

In 1991 the Scottish Education Department distributed to all Scottish schools a set of twelve 'ethos indicators'. One of the ways of introducing these to a School Board (or Board of Governors) is with the following simple instrument containing the 12 ethos categories.

Purpose

The purpose of the instrument is to begin the process of reflection and debate about ethos, what its constituent parts are and how the school might obtain evidence as to the quality and improvement of its ethos.

Use

Each member of the group (it need not be a Board) is asked to choose five of the indicators which they see as most important and prioritise them from 1 to 5, writing the relevant number in each box under the heading 'my view'. Group members then work in groups of three and try to reach agreement on their top five and the ordering of them. They then come back into the whole group and repeat the exercise, once more trying to reach consensus. They may ultimately agree to differ and say that it is hard to prioritise, but it is the process of discussion which helps to clarify concepts, differing viewpoints and issues around important priorities for the school.

THE **SELF-EVALUATION** FILE

ETHOS INDICATORS	My view	Small group view	Board view
Pupil morale			
Teacher morale			
Teacher job satisfaction			
The physical environment			
The learning context			
Teacher-pupil relationships			
Discipline			
Equality and justice			
Extra-curricular activities			
School leadership			
Information to parents			
Parent-teacher consultation			

ETHOS - A PRIMARY EXAMPLE

These instruments were developed by teachers in a primary school in Scotland, (Coalsnaughton). One is for use by pupils and the other for parents.

Use

It is important to create the climate in which pupils are encouraged to give their own view and to be reassured that teachers want to know what they really think and that pupils shouldn't put their names on the form.

Parents too need to be reassured that their views are given in confidence.

Being invited to give their views is likely to raise expectations that something will be done as a consequence, so it important to let people know beforehand what the limitations are.

That is:

- Views will be different. Not everyone will agree
- Some things may lend themselves to immediate action
- Some things will need to be addressed in the longer term
- Some things may be beyond the powers of the school to do anything about
- Pupils and parents will be given results of the survey

THE **SELF-EVALUATION** FILE

Pupil's Questionnaire

Here is a list of things that describes a school and the things which happen in this school.
Is this school a lot like your school, quite like your school or not like your school at all?

The School	A lot like my school	quite like my school	Not like my school
1. Pupils don't run in the corridors.			
2. Pupils say "good morning" to the teachers and visitors when they meet them.			
3. Pupils are always rude and shout to each other.			
4. Pupils are proud of their school.			
5. The teachers are usually smiling, and friendly to the pupils.			
6. The pupils like to talk to the teachers.			
7. Pupils always push and shove each other in the corridors			
8. Pupils are generally well behaved.			
9. The school is always a very loud, noisy place.			
10. Visitors get a friendly welcome.			
11. Parents like coming to the school.			
12. The head teacher doesn't often speak to the pupils.			
13. Pupils can push their way to be first in the line.			
14. The school is cold and uncomfortable.			
15. The school is clean and tidy.			
16. The school is a happy place to be in.			

THE **SELF-EVALUATION** FILE

Parents' Questionnaire

1) How many children to you have at the school? (Please tick.)

    1 ☐   2 ☐   3 ☐   4 ☐

2) Please tick which class/classes your child/children are in.

    1/2 ☐   2/3 ☐   4/5 ☐   6/7 ☐

Headteacher	Strongly Agree	Agree	Disagree	Strongly Disagree
1. The school makes me feel welcome.				
2. I am happy to meet the headteacher.				
3. The headteacher will listen to my concerns.				
4. I know my discussions with the headteacher will be treated confidentially				
5. I am confident my child is treated fairly by the headteacher.				
6. I feel the headteacher knows my child personally.				
7. My child thinks the headteacher is a friendly person.				
8. The headteacher has a pleasant and friendly manner.				

Comments

Classteachers				
1. The teachers in the school are friendly.				
2. I am happy to approach my child's classteacher.				
3. The classteacher will listen to my concerns.				
4. I know my discussions with the classteacher will be treated confidentially				
5. I am confident that my child is treated fairly by his/her classteacher.				

THE **SELF-EVALUATION** FILE

3. THE CHANGE PROFILE

A variant on the ethos indicator instrument is the change profile, developed for use in the Improving School Effectiveness Project in Scotland. It was used with groups of teachers and senior management to evaluate their school, providing a baseline at a given point in time and then again one or two years later.

Purpose

The purpose is to engage a critical conversation on key aspects of school culture in which, with the support of a critical friend or consultant, there is a press for evidence and recognition of the desire to inquire further and deeper into those aspects of culture with a view to continuous improvement.

Use

A group comes together - ideally 4-6, and goes systematically through each item trying to come to consensus on how they would rate the school. At each stage the chair, facilitator, or critical friend should be pressing for evidence with questions such as 'How do we know that? What other sources of evidence might we look for?

THE **SELF-EVALUATION** FILE

CHANGE PROFILE:
CONDITIONS FOR SCHOOL IMPROVEMENT

Pupil learning is likely to be enhanced when the following statements apply:

1. This is a learning school

There is a commitment by staff to reflect, to adapt and to learn. This expresses itself in staff dealings with one another, with pupils and parents. People are not afraid to try something new and are encouraged to experiment.

2. There are high expectations of pupil achievement.

There is a widely shared commitment to high achievement. Staff believe that all children can surpass their own, teachers' and parents' expectations. Efforts are made to share that conviction with the pupil and parent body and to realise it in a range of practical ways. There is a belief that all teachers can and must make a difference to children's learning.

3. There is ownership of change.

People behave proactively rather than reactively. They initiate change in a way designed to further the main purpose of the school rather than simply responding to imposed change from the outside. It is a common assumption that no matter how effective the school is, more can always be achieved.

4. There are widely shared goals and values.

There is shared understanding of the school's values and priorities and shared commitment to its core values. This is important at the level of teaching staff but should be extended to support staff and, as far as possible, to parents and pupils and other key players. There is talk about 'what is important in this school' as part of an ongoing process of self-evaluation and development.

5. There is effective communication

Members of the immediate school community (plus parents and others in the wider community) are kept informed; are confident that their information is acted upon and that their views are heard by the school. People feel free to speak their mind.

6. Pupil learning is a major focus of attention

In the forefront of the school's planning, innovation and change is a concern for pupil learning. It is manifested in day-to-day dialogue among staff and in pupil-staff and staff-parent relationships.

7. Leadership is effective

There is confidence in those who make key decisions about the vision and direction of the school. They are able to recruit and motivate people and foster a culture open to change and learning.

8. There is real home-school partnership

Staff believe that parents have a key role to play in supporting pupil learning; and in the school in general. Staff and management make efforts to inform and involve parents on a collaborative basis.

9. Relationships are based on respect for individuals

There is a high level of mutual respect among staff for one another's professionality and for the integrity of the individual. All are seen as having something to offer. Respect for the individual is also demonstrated in staff dealings with pupils and parents. Recognition and celebration of differences and different achievements are highlighted. Diversity is seen as a strength. There are high levels of mutual trust.

10. Collaboration and partnership are a way of life

People work together. There is a consistent approach which is supportive. People are not left to sink or swim. People are available to help each other. Team teaching, mentoring, peer coaching, joint planning and mutual observation and feedback are a normal part of the everyday life of the school.

THE CHANGE PROFILE

Circle the number which shows what you think.

1 = very like our school   -   4 = not at all like our school

This is a learning school	1	2	3	4
There are high expectations of pupil achievement	1	2	3	4
There is ownership of change	1	2	3	4
There are widely shared goals and values	1	2	3	4
There is effective communication	1	2	3	4
Pupil learning is a major focus of attention	1	2	3	4
Leadership is effective	1	2	3	4
There is real home-school partnership	1	2	3	4
Relationships are based on respect for individuals	1	2	3	4
Collaboration and partnership are a way of life	1	2	3	4

THE **SELF-EVALUATION** FILE

4. ETHOS IN A WORD

This instrument is used to give a profile of school ethos as seen from the point of view of teachers, pupils, parents or any other stakeholders whose views may be sought. The user simply goes down the list scoring 1 to 5 on each of the characteristics. Room is provided at the end to add one or more descriptors of your own.

tidy	1	2	3	4	5	untidy
warm	1	2	3	4	5	cold
parent-friendly	1	2	3	4	5	parent-unfriendly
colourful	1	2	3	4	5	drab
authoritarian	1	2	3	4	5	democratic
comfortable	1	2	3	4	5	uncomfortable
orderly	1	2	3	4	5	disorderly
sensitive	1	2	3	4	5	insensitive
strict	1	2	3	4	5	easy-going
high stress	1	2	3	4	5	low stress
pessimistic	1	2	3	4	5	optimistic
tense	1	2	3	4	5	relaxed
helpful	1	2	3	4	5	unhelpful
competitive	1	2	3	4	5	uncompetitive
formal	1	2	3	4	5	informal
reactive	1	2	3	4	5	proactive
likes change	1	2	3	4	5	dislikes change
stimulating	1	2	3	4	5	boring
pupil-friendly	1	2	3	4	5	pupil-unfriendly
inflexible	1	2	3	4	5	flexible
clear values	1	2	3	4	5	no clear values
avoids conflict	1	2	3	4	5	responds well to conflict
adventurous	1	2	3	4	5	cautious
uses time well	1	2	3	4	5	time used badly
risk-taking	1	2	3	4	5	avoids risks
open to new ideas	1	2	3	4	5	sceptical of new ideas
idealistic	1	2	3	4	5	pragmatic
pursues long term goals	1	2	3	4	5	pursues short term goals
looks to the past	1	2	3	4	5	looks to the future
....	1	2	3	4	5	....

THE SELF-EVALUATION FILE

5. THE SELF-EVALUATION PROFILE

Purpose

The self-evaluation profile (SEP) is an instrument designed for use by teachers, parents, pupils and school management as a simple but highly effective introduction to school self-evaluating. Its origins lie in a European project which involved 101 schools in 18 countries all of whom agreed to use the SEP and to follow the process outlined below.

Use

Step 1
The school composes small groups of teachers, parents, pupils and School Board/governors.

Step 2
Each of these groups are given copies of the SEP and go through it systematically scoring each item on a four point scale (from double plus to double minus) and trying to reach agreement as a group on each of the twelve items. Groups are encouraged to seek and respect evidence in coming to their conclusion.

Step 3.
Each group sends a representative to the school evaluation group. This should consist of not more than ten people, 2-3 pupils, 2 teachers, 2 parents, 2 board members and a member of school senior management. This large group goes through the SEP again item by item trying to reach consensus but pressing for evidence to justify their judgement.

THE **SELF-EVALUATION** FILE

Step 4.

The group agree on one or two key areas to explore in greater depth over the coming year or term.

The process

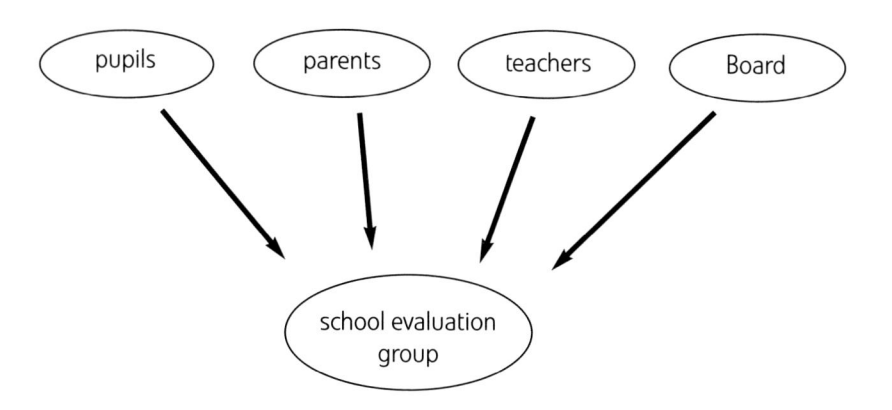

```
   pupils      parents      teachers      Board
      \          |            /            /
       \         |           /            /
        \        ↓          ↓            /
         ↓                               ↓
              school evaluation
                   group
```

THE SELF-EVALUATION FILE

THE SEP

	++	+	-	--	⇩	⇔	⇧

Outcomes

academic achievement							
personal and social development							
student destinations							

Process at classroom level

time for learning							
quality of learning and teaching							
support for learning difficulties							

Process at school level

school as a learning place							
school as a social place							
school as a professional place							

Environment

school and home							
school and community							
school and work							

THE SELF-EVALUATION FILE

6. THE DOUBLE-SIDED QUESTIONNAIRE

Purpose

The double-sided questionnaire is used to give two sets of views of schools and classrooms, contrasting what people see as desirable with what they see as actually happening - expectations measured against satisfaction. The gap between the two provides a graphic view of issues that a school needs to pay attention to, open for discussion, and build into future planning.

Use

The questionnaire may be used with teachers, pupils, parents, indeed any group whose views are seen as important and influential. The questionnaire may be customised to meet different purposes. The example below illustrates the typical double-sided structure while the following page contains a blank form into which items may be entered.

the school now	the effective school
1 = strongly agree	1 = crucial
2 = agree	2 = very important
3 = uncertain	3 = quite important
4 = disagree	4 = not very important
5 = strongly disagree	5 = not at all important

1 2 3 4 5	Pupils respect teachers in this school	1 2 3 4 5
1 2 3 4 5	Teachers believe that all children in this school can be successful	1 2 3 4 5
1 2 3 4 5	Teachers regularly discuss ways of improving pupils' learning	1 2 3 4 5
1 2 3 4 5	Teachers regularly observe each other in the classroom and give feedback	1 2 3 4 5
1 2 3 4 5	Standards set for pupils are consistently upheld across the school	1 2 3 4 5
1 2 3 4 5	Teachers share similar beliefs and attitudes about effective teaching/learning	1 2 3 4 5

THE **SELF-EVALUATION** FILE

1 2 3 4 5		1 2 3 4 5
1 2 3 4 5		1 2 3 4 5
1 2 3 4 5		1 2 3 4 5
1 2 3 4 5		1 2 3 4 5
1 2 3 4 5		1 2 3 4 5
1 2 3 4 5		1 2 3 4 5
1 2 3 4 5		1 2 3 4 5
1 2 3 4 5		1 2 3 4 5
1 2 3 4 5		1 2 3 4 5
1 2 3 4 5		1 2 3 4 5
1 2 3 4 5		1 2 3 4 5
1 2 3 4 5		1 2 3 4 5
1 2 3 4 5		1 2 3 4 5
1 2 3 4 5		1 2 3 4 5
1 2 3 4 5		1 2 3 4 5
1 2 3 4 5		1 2 3 4 5
1 2 3 4 5		1 2 3 4 5
1 2 3 4 5		1 2 3 4 5

THE **SELF-EVALUATION** FILE

7. SHOWING THE GAP

The following is one way of comparing importance and satisfaction and representing the gap.

Comparison of teachers' rating of importance and actuality

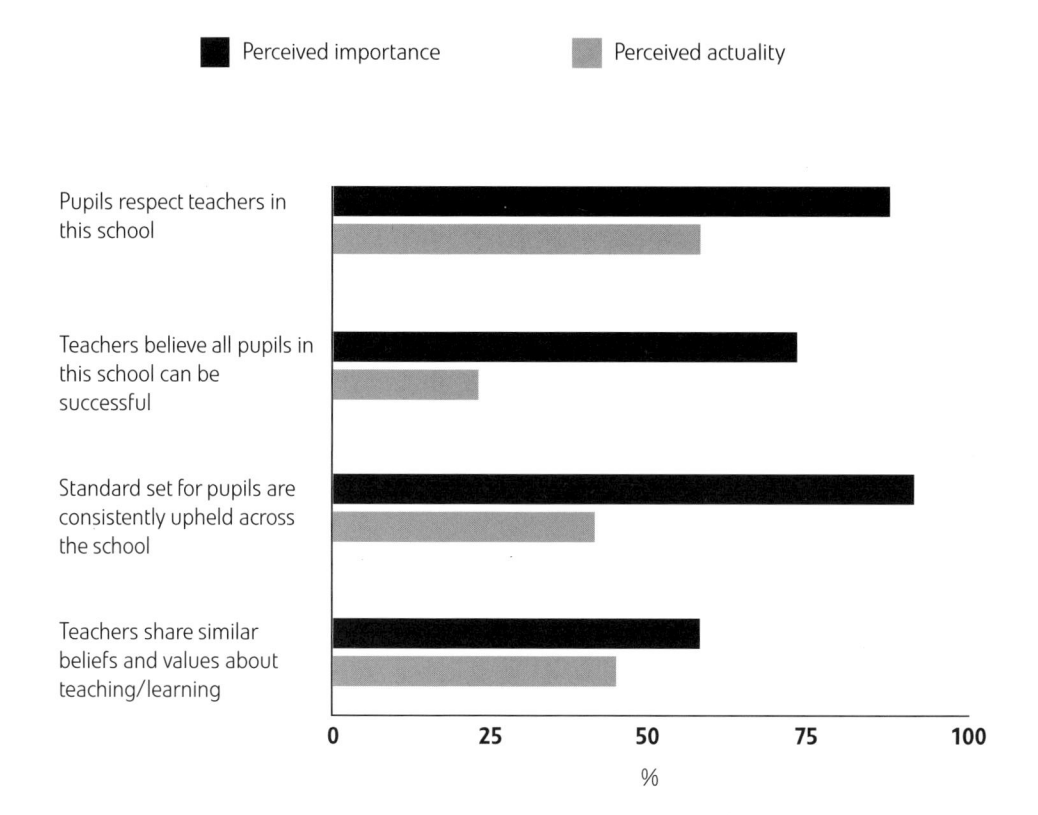

■ Perceived importance   ▨ Perceived actuality

Pupils respect teachers in this school

Teachers believe all pupils in this school can be successful

Standard set for pupils are consistently upheld across the school

Teachers share similar beliefs and values about teaching/learning

0   25   50   75   100
%

8. TRIANGULATION

Using the same items with a number of different response groups allows comparisons to be made, serving as a basis for discussion and development within the school. The first example compares teachers', pupils' and parents' responses on the same items.

% agree/strongly agree	teachers	pupils	parents
I enjoy school, My child enjoys school, Pupils enjoy school	58	83	90
Pupils respect teachers in this school	78	72	71
Homework is interesting and useful	80	50	61
There is good order and discipline in the school	71	61	58
Pupils with learning difficulties get help and support	81	80	78
Pupils have a say in school development planning	29	19	?
Pupils work together and help each other	77	77	81

THE **SELF-EVALUATION** FILE

This second example compares responses at three levels within the school - teachers, middle management and senior management.

% agree/strongly agree

	teachers	middle managers	senior managers
senior staff are available to discuss curriculum and teaching matters	62	73	92
the SMT openly recognises teachers when they do things well	26	35	71
there is mutual respect between staff and SMT in this school	54	50	69
staff feel encouraged to bring forward new ideas	51	56	79
decision-making processes are fair	41	46	79
staff participate in important decision-making	29	38	80
there is effective communication between SMT and teachers	46	48	87

In all the examples given above the power of these data lies in opening up issues for discussion, It is easy to get caught up with the numbers and discussions about statistics. That is not the purpose or value of the exercise. Its purpose is to consider why people might hold different perceptions, to openly and non-defensively explore different explanations, to consider what might be done to communicate more effectively, to share feelings more openly, and jointly to discuss ways of making the school a more satisfying and effective place for everyone.

THE **SELF-EVALUATION** FILE

9. BENCHMARKING ETHOS

When a number of schools agree to use the same questionnaire items comparisons can be made across schools, individual school data going back to the school together with data for all schools . This allows for a form of benchmarking.

AGREE   **CRUCIAL**

your school	all schools		your school	all schools
58%	48%	Pupils respect teachers in this school	95%	95%
16%	31%	Teachers believe that all children in this school can be successful	70%	75%
58%	58%	Teachers regularly discuss ways of improving pupils learning	91%	93%
38%	7%	Teachers regularly observe each other in the classroom and give feedback	51%	31%
33%	19%	Standards set for pupils are consistently upheld across the school	96%	93%
35%	22%	Teachers share similar beliefs and attitudes about effective teaching/learning	55%	60%
57%	48%	Staff have a commitment to the whole school and not just their class or department	87%	88%

While comparing like with like is always useful in benchmarking, comparing like with unlike can also present a challenge, as the following example of a secondary benchmarking against primary school data shows:

prim	sec		prim	sec
61%	31%	Teachers believe that all children in this school can be successful	87%	75%
72%	48%	Staff have a commitment to the whole school and not just their class or department	96%	88%

To be able to do this does imply that schools have agreed to embark on an evaluation exercise together and have committed themselves to sharing their data with another, This is normally done through a project, perhaps in conjunction with a university, the local authority or as part of a Government sponsored initiative.

THE **SELF-EVALUATION** FILE

SECTION 3

MANAGEMENT AND LEADERSHIP

This section contains a collection of instruments which can be used by school leaders to evaluate themselves and/or be evaluated by others. While it is not easy in practice to separate management from leadership, the conceptual distinction between the two is important and discussion of the concepts is a useful prelude to evaluation.

It can be helpful for people to think through these issues for themselves, putting into one box those things that fall most easily into 'management' and those that are more clearly 'leadership'.

MANAGEMENT	LEADERSHIP

THE **SELF-EVALUATION** FILE

The following is an example from one school:

MANAGEMENT	LEADERSHIP
• Resourcing • Timetabling • Keeping the financial accounts • Attending council meetings • Chairing meetings effectively • Ensuring information flow to School Board • Delegating responsibility to appropriate staff • Keeping up to date with information and policy development • Keeping support staff in the picture	• Working with staff on a vision statement • Helping people to set goals and targets for themselves • Encouraging the leadership of others • Listening to teachers' concerns • Supporting staff with difficulties • Engaging other community agencies in the work of the school • Putting important things first • Walking the talk • Making quality time for parents

THE **SELF-EVALUATION** FILE

1. ME AS I AM/ME AS I WOULD LIKE TO BE

This instrument, similar in design to the 'Ethos in a word' (page 60) but in this case is concerned with personal and professional qualities that underpin management and leadership. The protocol comes in two parts which are best tackled sequentially - first, a reflection on 'me as I am' (or how I see myself) before reflecting on the qualities that 'I' aspire to.

Purpose

The instrument is best used in a collegial context as a prompt to discussion, comparing notes and providing a prelude to mentoring, coaching or other ways of working on the gap between who I am and who I aspire to be. It may be returned to at different points over time to consider change and growth.

Use

The individual (head, teacher, authority adviser, inspector) fills out *Me as I am*, going down the list circling the item which provides the closest fit. He/she then connects the circles to give a profile (heavy marker pen is preferable) . He/she then repeats the process with 'Me as I would like to be', again ending up with a profile in marker pen. The two sheets may then be overlaid to match and held up to the light to get a quick view of the gap.

When people do this in a group they may pair and share or the group may open up discussion around the items. This does not require that people disclose what they have written - although they may volunteer to do so - but to discuss issues that are raised by the exercise. Such discussions typically refer to the context in which the qualities are relevant. In other words these are not necessarily static personal attributes but highly context dependent. This is an important insight to pursue in discussion because it helps to develop thinking about what is appropriate in different situations and what is more likely to be effective in different circumstances and in different relationships. This helps to dispel fixed views about qualities or 'competencies' as individual personality traits and shift the focus to situations, climate, contexts which encourage or discourage certain kinds of behaviour.

It is instructive to ask someone to go through the same items from an outside perspective 'You as You are' from my point of view. This does require a high degree of trust and willingness to learn.

THE **SELF-EVALUATION** FILE

ME AS I AM

rule breaker	1	2	3	4	5	rule observer
efficient	1	2	3	4	5	inefficient
radical	1	2	3	4	5	conservative
share power	1	2	3	4	5	hold power
authoritarian	1	2	3	4	5	democratic
charismatic	1	2	3	4	5	reserved
pursue long term goals	1	2	3	4	5	pursue short term goals
forgiving	1	2	3	4	5	unforgiving
competitive	1	2	3	4	5	uncompetitive
delegate a lot	1	2	3	4	5	delegate very little
like change	1	2	3	4	5	dislike change
confront bad practice	1	2	3	4	5	tolerate bad practice
gentle	1	2	3	4	5	tough
reliable	1	2	3	4	5	erratic
strong values	1	2	3	4	5	open-minded
attend to detail	1	2	3	4	5	careless about detail
gregarious	1	2	3	4	5	private
size up people well	1	2	3	4	5	bad at sizing up people
demanding	1	2	3	4	5	undemanding
individualistic	1	2	3	4	5	team player
inflexible	1	2	3	4	5	flexible
optimist	1	2	3	4	5	pessimist
fight for beliefs	1	2	3	4	5	back off from a fight
entrepreneurial	1	2	3	4	5	cautious
predictable	1	2	3	4	5	unpredictable
take risks	1	2	3	4	5	avoid risks
take decisions easily	1	2	3	4	5	difficulty in decision-making
assertive	1	2	3	4	5	unassertive
manipulative	1	2	3	4	5	straightforward
easily influenced	1	2	3	4	5	unbending
low profile	1	2	3	4	5	high profile
idealistic	1	2	3	4	5	pragmatic
listen more than talk	1	2	3	4	5	talk more than listen
lead from the front	1	2	3	4	5	lead from the back
intuitive	1	2	3	4	5	logical
…………………………	1	2	3	4	5	…………………

THE **SELF-EVALUATION** FILE

ME AS I WOULD LIKE TO BE

rule breaker	1	2	3	4	5	rule observer
efficient	1	2	3	4	5	inefficient
radical	1	2	3	4	5	conservative
share power	1	2	3	4	5	hold power
authoritarian	1	2	3	4	5	democratic
charismatic	1	2	3	4	5	reserved
forgiving	1	2	3	4	5	unforgiving
competitive	1	2	3	4	5	uncompetitive
delegate a lot	1	2	3	4	5	delegate very little
like change	1	2	3	4	5	dislike change
confront bad practice	1	2	3	4	5	tolerate bad practice
gentle	1	2	3	4	5	tough
reliable	1	2	3	4	5	erratic
strong values	1	2	3	4	5	open-minded
attend to detail	1	2	3	4	5	careless about detail
gregarious	1	2	3	4	5	private
size up people well	1	2	3	4	5	bad at sizing up people
demanding	1	2	3	4	5	undemanding
individualistic	1	2	3	4	5	team player
inflexible	1	2	3	4	5	flexible
optimist	1	2	3	4	5	pessimist
fight for beliefs	1	2	3	4	5	back off from a fight
entrepreunerial	1	2	3	4	5	cautious
predictable	1	2	3	4	5	unpredictable
pursue long term goals	1	2	3	4	5	pursue short term goals
take risks	1	2	3	4	5	avoid risks
take decisions easily	1	2	3	4	5	difficulty in decision-making
assertive	1	2	3	4	5	unassertive
manipulative	1	2	3	4	5	straightforward
easily influenced	1	2	3	4	5	unbending
low profile	1	2	3	4	5	high profile
idealistic	1	2	3	4	5	pragmatic
listen more than talk	1	2	3	4	5	talk more than listen
lead from the front	1	2	3	4	5	lead from the back
intuitive	1	2	3	4	5	logical

2. PIE CHARTS

The pie charts (or 'pi' chart) is the simplest of all devices and can take less than a minute to complete but is potentially powerful in the discussion which it generates.

Purpose

Its purpose is to provide a quick and easy way of getting into far-reaching issues in leadership and management style. It provides the starting point for an ongoing dialogue and development process affecting everyone in the school.

Use

The school principal draws three lines within the circle to represent how he/she sees the balance of command, consultation and consensus in decision-making in his/her school. This may be followed by one or all of the following:

- Private reflection on whether this balance is satisfying and how it might be justified
- Discussing it with an adviser or critical friend
- Asking someone else (e.g. another member of the senior management to complete it as he/she perceives your decision-making
- Asking members of the staff to provide their perception of decision-making in the school
- Discussion of what kinds of activities should come within each of these three categories

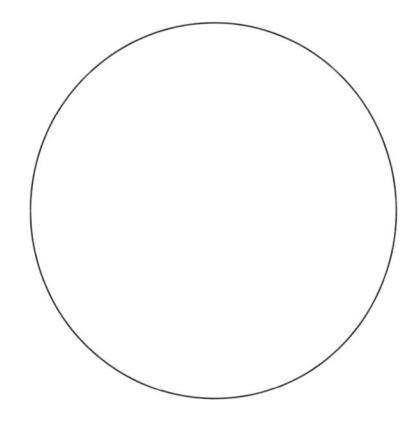

THE **SELF-EVALUATION** FILE

As people engage in this exercise they usually find that the classification into three categories depends on a whole range of factors such as the type of decision involved, the context (time of year, length of time the head has been in the school, familiarity with staff, the morale of teachers.

The questions thrown up by the exercise, when brought into the open for discussion, allow a closer examination of policy and policy in practice. This can be handled sensitively, help to dispel resentment and grievances about decision-making and provide valuable guidance for development planning.

The following overall balance, suggested by some researchers as optimum for a healthy culture, does provide a kind of benchmark against which to judge practice.

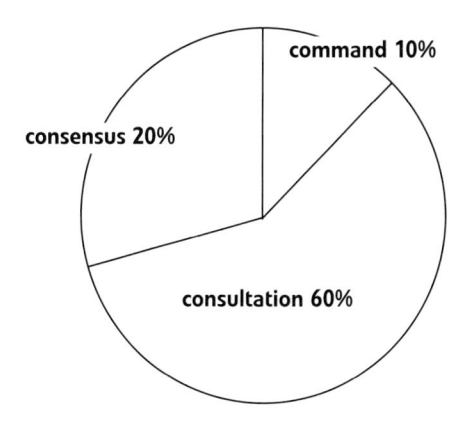

command 10%
consensus 20%
consultation 60%

3. THE HEADTEACHER'S 24 HOUR LOG

The log is a way of recording events, decisions, aims and values within a very specific time frame, for example one day or one week. It may be used by anyone in the school, including students, but in this case is focused on management and leadership.

Purpose

The purpose is to provide a fairly objective documentation of how a headteacher spends his/her time, setting that against the priorities and values he/she espouses. In other words, 'espoused theory' and 'theory-in-use'.

Use

The user agrees to fill this in conscientiously over the course of one day (or more as agreed) noting the time spent, the people and the place (e.g. 8.00-8.23 talking to a parent in my office). The outcome, however inconsequential, is noted as well as the perceived purpose of the event or interaction.

The follow up is to compare these data with the headteacher's expression of values and his/her perception of time management. So before completing the log (shown overleaf) it is important that he/she fills in the form on values and time estimates.

THE **SELF-EVALUATION** FILE

Time	Where	With whom?	With what outcome?	With what purpose?

Before completing the log it is important that the individual fills in the following form, comprising a reflection on values and priorities and a 'guesstimate' of how his/her time is divided. The evidence from the log may then constitute a surprise and require a rethink, perhaps of values and priorities, perhaps of management of time.

What is important...

To me?

To teachers?

To pupils?

To the school?

How do I spend my time?

Where?

Who with?

With what outcome?

With what purpose?

THE SELF-EVALUATION FILE

4. THE URGENCY/IMPORTANCE MATRIX

Reflection on time management and priorities lends itself to the well-known urgent/important matrix. This asks leaders and managers to categorise into four quadrants the urgent and the important. This may be done in the form of four in-baskets.

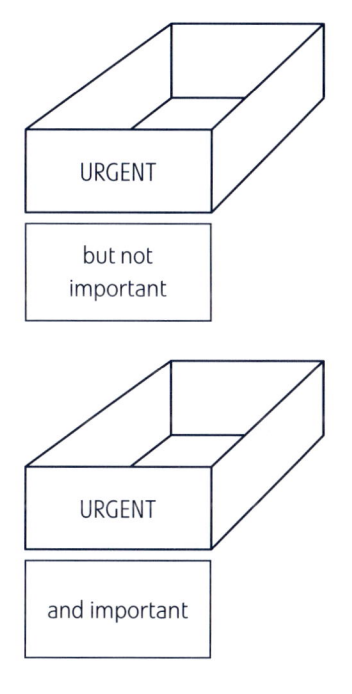

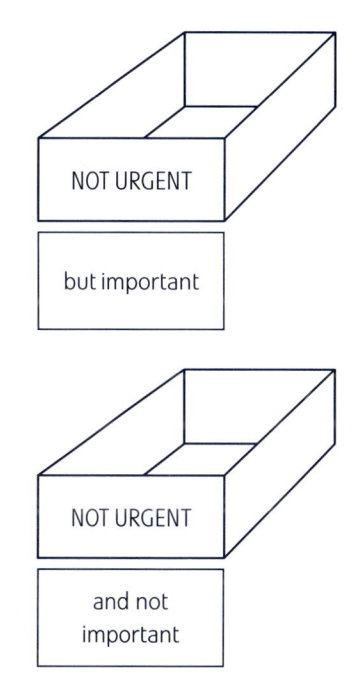

URGENT — but not important

NOT URGENT — but important

URGENT — and important

NOT URGENT — and not important

The content of these four boxes or 'quadrants' may be represented as below:

Quadrant 1
crises
pressing problems
deadline-driven
projects and meetings

Quadrant 2
preparation
prevention
values clarification
relationship building
empowerment
relaxation

Quadrant 3
needless interruptions
unimportant meetings,
phone calls
other people's minor issues

Quadrant 4
trivia, busywork
time wasters
escape activities
irrelevant mail
excessive relaxation

THE **SELF-EVALUATION** FILE

Purpose

This may be used by a member of the senior management team, middle management, or by teachers, to examine how they order priorities and manage time for the important things.

Use

The individual reconsiders tasks lying ahead over the course of the following day or week. He/she then 'puts' these task into one of four boxes. This may take the form of simply writing in four boxes on a squared piece of paper. These are then reviewed to see what things might be put into a different box. It may be useful then to share this with another member of staff or critical friend.

Example

The following is an example of what one member of a senior management team wrote:

Quadrant 1
'demand' by Frank to see me immediately (4th time this week)

deadline for tender (4th tender this month)

return phone call to suppliers

accept invitation to speak at management conference

Quadrant 2
classroom observation - JK

visit by Dutch principals

disciplinary hearing on Website misuse

staff meeting

phone architects

answer emails

order self-evaluation file

Quadrant 3
Meeting with Mrs Shastra about her son being bullied (racism?)

change date for advisory meeting

lunch time supervision

talk to Phillip (Y7) about his behaviour

Quadrant 4
lunch with Kay

article for MST

KS2/3 conference

reading departmental circulars

junk mail

5. HOW GOOD IS LEADERSHIP IN OUR SCHOOL?

This example comes from the Scottish Executive Education Department and their self-evaluation guidelines "How Good is our School? The guidelines cover different aspects of school quality and effectiveness including management and leadership. It asks schools to evaluate themselves on the same 4 point scale used by the inspectorate, providing two exemplars and allowing school themselves to complement these with their own level 1 and 3 descriptors.

Level 4 - Illustration

- He or she demonstrates a high level of professional competence and commitment based on wide-ranging up-to-date knowledge and skills, including the ability to initiate, direct, communicate, manage staff and their development and delegate effectively. Where applicable, his or her teaching is a model of good practice.

- He or she has a wide range of relevant personal qualities, including the ability to create confidence and inspire others; he or she is a positive influence on his or her area of responsibility. He or she has the ability to evaluate objectively the qualities of staff and their contributions to teamwork. He or she demonstrates breadth of vision and can take difficult decisions effectively when necessary.

- He or she has very good relationships with pupils, parents and staff. There is a planned development of teamwork, staff are involved in policy development and his or her dissemination of information is clear and prompt.

A performance broadly equivalent to that illustrated above would merit a Level 4 award.

THE **SELF-EVALUATION** FILE

Level 2 Illustration

- He or she demonstrates a degree of professional competence based on relevant knowledge, although this is not always successfully applied in practical contexts. There are difficulties in communicating and/or delegating effectively and attempts at initiating and directing are only partially effective. Where applicable, their teaching provides a good model in a number of respects.

- He or she demonstrates leadership but is not wholly successful in inspiring confidence in others and a number of staff do not respond to his or her management style, either because he or she is not wholly successful in inspiring confidence or does not provide a clear sense of direction. He or she lacks breadth of vision and tends to avoid difficult decisions.

- Difficulties arise at times in his or her relationships with pupils, staff and/or parents. He or she has difficulties at times in creating a team approach and while there are attempts to do so, in practice there are only occasional instances of effective teamwork and dissemination of information is not always clear or prompt.

A performance broadly equivalent to that illustrated above would merit a Level 2 award.

THE SELF-EVALUATION FILE

6. HOW GOOD AM I AS A LEADER AND MANAGER?

The descriptors may be translated into a self-evaluation profile such as the one below. The fifth column asks for a judgement, whether in the user's view this constitutes a leadership or management quality?

Qualities of Leadership	1	2	3	4	M or L
Professional competence and commitment					
Commitment					
Up-to-date knowledge					
Ability to initiate					
Ability to direct					
Communication skills					
Manage staff effectively					
Support staff development					
Delegates effectively					
Models good teacher					
Leadership qualities					
Creates confidence in others					
Inspires others					
Has a positive impact on practice					
Ability to evaluate others effectively					
Demonstrates breadth of vision					
Takes decisions effectively					
Relationship with people and deployment of teamwork					
Maintains good relationships with staff					
Maintains good relationships with pupils					
Maintains good relationships with parents					
Involves others in policy development					
Disseminates information promptly and effectively					

THE **SELF-EVALUATION** FILE

7. FORMAL AND INFORMAL LEADERSHIP

Leadership in a school is not always located at the apex of the organisation nor with specific high status individuals. Leadership is usually more complex and diffuse and shared among different 'players' in a school.

Purpose

This simple instrument is designed to encourage teachers and students and parents too to examine more closely and critically what leadership means in practice, where it can be found in the informal day-to-day life of the school, who exercises it in an ascribed role or informally and self, or group, appointed.

Distributed leadership' - with whom and where it is located

Formal	Informal

THE **SELF-EVALUATION** FILE

Example

Here are some the things that one working group wrote

Formal	Informal
SMT	Mark Brown - highly regarded by colleagues
J.K - union rep	Pamela Tymms, NQT - brilliant innovator
Heads of Department	Curtis Taylor pupil Y9 - school ICT expert
Yashida- study support co-ordinator	Valerie Small , pupil Y10- innovator and leader of Aerobics club
PP - runs highly successful netball team	Joe Lawton, caretaker, constant source of good ideas
Anouka - Head girl	Anne, senior teacher - organises brilliant CPD sessions
Leonard T. - chair of governors	
Betty Barclay - school secretary	
Madeleine T. - chairs cross-curricular working party	

Indicators, benchmarks etc.

Indicators, benchmarks and targets are not in the common vocabulary of schools. These terms are often confused, however. It can be a useful exercise for staff to clarify their understandings of these terms by working as a group filling in the relevant boxes.

	Indicator	Benchmark	Target
Definition			
Example			

THE **SELF-EVALUATION** FILE

Indicators, benchmarks and targets – a flow chart

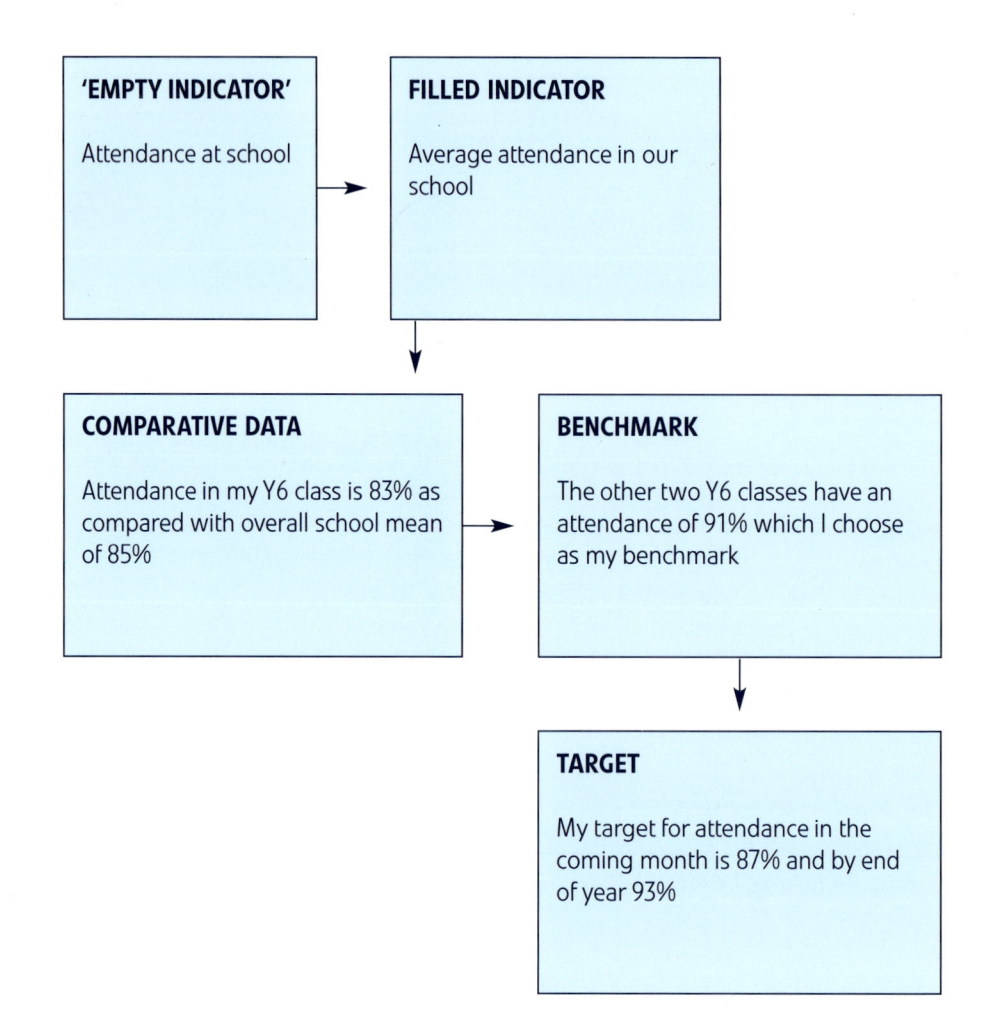

'EMPTY INDICATOR'

Attendance at school

→

FILLED INDICATOR

Average attendance in our school

↓

COMPARATIVE DATA

Attendance in my Y6 class is 83% as compared with overall school mean of 85%

→

BENCHMARK

The other two Y6 classes have an attendance of 91% which I choose as my benchmark

↓

TARGET

My target for attendance in the coming month is 87% and by end of year 93%